T0294518

# Creating Great
# Visitor Experiences

## AMERICAN ALLIANCE OF MUSEUMS

The American Alliance of Museums has been bringing museums together since 1906, helping to develop standards and best practices, gathering and sharing knowledge, and providing advocacy on issues of concern to the entire museum community. Representing more than 35,000 individual museum professionals and volunteers, institutions, and corporate partners serving the museum field, the Alliance stands for the broad scope of the museum community.

The American Alliance of Museums' mission is to champion museums and nurture excellence in partnership with its members and allies.

Books published by AAM further the Alliance's mission to make standards and best practices for the broad museum community widely available.

# Creating Great Visitor Experiences

## A Guide for Museum Professionals

Colleen Higginbotham

ROWMAN & LITTLEFIELD
*Lanham • Boulder • New York • London*

Published by Rowman & Littlefield
An imprint of The Rowman & Littlefield Publishing Group, Inc.
4501 Forbes Boulevard, Suite 200, Lanham, Maryland 20706
www.rowman.com

86-90 Paul Street, London EC2A 4NE

British Library Cataloguing in Publication Information Available

**Library of Congress Cataloging-in-Publication Data**

Names: Higginbotham, Colleen, 1977– author. | American Alliance of Museums.
Title: Creating great visitor experiences : a guide for museum
  professionals / Colleen Higginbotham.
Description: Lanham : Rowman & Littlefield, [2022] | Includes
  bibliographical references and index. | Summary: "Creating Great Visitor
  Experiences: A Guide for Museum Professionals will help museums define
  their service, hire and train a dynamic frontline team, and spread a
  culture of service throughout their institution"— Provided by
  publisher.
Identifiers: LCCN 2022016746 (print) | LCCN 2022016747 (ebook) | ISBN
  9781538150214 (cloth) | ISBN 9781538150221 (paperback) | ISBN
  9781538150238 (epub)
Subjects: LCSH: Museums—United States—Management. | Museum
  visitors—United States. | Museums—United States—Social aspects. |
  Museums—United States—Educational aspects.
Classification: LCC AM121 .H54 2022  (print) | LCC AM121  (ebook) | DDC
  069/.1—dc23/eng/20220603
LC record available at https://lccn.loc.gov/2022016746
LC ebook record available at https://lccn.loc.gov/2022016747

This book is dedicated to the talented and enthusiastic frontline team members at museums around the world, particularly the incredible gallery hosts at the Chrysler Museum of Art. You are ambassadors who are making a difference with museum visitors every day.

# Contents

# Foreword

The Chrysler Museum of Art is known for its outstanding collections of paintings, sculptures, glass, and photographs, but the art is just one part of the whole. The welcoming and inclusive quality of the visitor experience defines the ethos of the institution as much as any masterpiece or set of objects. It is our intent to bring art and people together to foster a meaningful engagement. The riches of our collection are there to be enjoyed by all.

A visit to the Chrysler begins with a friendly gallery host opening the front door and inviting you inside. The warm welcome continues throughout the museum as these hosts create a comfortable atmosphere, answer questions, and engage visitors in conversations about works of art. This welcoming environment creates opportunities for genuine connections with works of art.

These connections are central to our mission, but the commitment to our visitors extends beyond the gallery-host team and influences all areas of our operations. Visitors are a top consideration in exhibition design, program development, and institutional planning. Professionals throughout the institution consider the varying preferences of our visitors and customize experiences to suit their levels of expertise, interests, and engagement styles. We look for employees who are ready to meet visitors as they are, from the most sophisticated art lover to the neophyte. We provide texts that are smart, informative, and devoid of jargon. Representatives from the frontline team are included in planning discussions, and curators and educators are happy to share their expertise with their colleagues working in the galleries.

Museums are cultural leaders in their communities, and this comes with the responsibility of welcoming all members of the community, not just those who have traditionally felt comfortable visiting museums. For museum audiences to truly reflect their communities, most museums need to attract a more diverse audience, and an important step in achieving that goal is identifying and eliminating barriers for potential visitors. The Chrysler Museum of Art is proud to offer free admission to all, eliminating a financial barrier. If you understand and embrace the differences in your visitors, you can adapt your service and offer personalized experiences. These quality experiences can help break through social, physical, and intellectual barriers.

Some new visitors may need to feel specifically invited to the museum, and community-engagement initiatives can bring them to your museum through programs and partnerships.

A strong positive experience can help them feel welcome and increase the likelihood that they will return to the museum and share positive thoughts about their experiences with friends and family.

For two decades, the Chrysler Museum of Art has made a pointed effort to be a more welcoming museum for the community. This is evident in our gallery-host program, our free admission, our community-engagement efforts, and our exhibition and programming offerings. Over these years, our attendance has increased, and our audience has become more diverse. This is particularly true of our younger audience. I consistently hear positive feedback from donors and members of the public about their experiences at the museum. They feel a strong affinity for the museum and think of the Chrysler as "their" museum. The attention to the visitor experience is a strong component of these efforts and successes. We feel the model we have established could have resonance with other museums as they evolve to meet the needs of the next generation of museumgoers.

In *Creating Great Visitor Experiences: A Guide for Museum Professionals*, Colleen Higginbotham shares her expertise with museum colleagues. For fifteen years, she has been at the forefront of the Chrysler's efforts to create the ideal space to experience great art. She is uniquely positioned to help museums build strong frontline teams, provide outstanding training, and build a culture of service throughout their institutions.

Dr. Erik Neil
Director and CEO
Chrysler Museum of Art

# Preface

Museums have ambitious mission statements with goals such as enriching and transforming lives, inspiring children, connecting people to the museum's content, and being a vital part of the community.

That visitor-centric ambition often shows as museums make multiyear strategic plans, with objectives like growing and diversifying museum audiences, increasing visitor satisfaction, and engaging the community.

Prioritizing the visitor experience can help your museum achieve all the goals above. Our visitors add meaning to our museums, and we need to care for those visitors with the same dedication that we apply to the care of our collections.

Once museums have decided to prioritize the visitor experience, they may find they don't have the experience or resources to execute change in this area. They may have a leader in visitor services who is talented at providing service and coaching their team, but they have never been responsible for building a staffing structure or creating a training program. An executive director may see this as a priority but may not have a strong connection to the details of the daily visitor experience, and this may be outside their area of expertise. *Creating Great Visitor Experiences: A Guide for Museum Professionals* is designed to help these individuals, and their museums, create fantastic experiences for their visitors.

The first step in providing that great experience is to learn everything you can about your visitors. Chapters 2 and 3 will help you understand the individual backgrounds, motivations, and preferences of your audience. In chapter 4, you will work with your colleagues to understand how visitors move through your museum. With all this information, you can prepare your museum for the visitor experience and think through the comfort of your visitors and your amenities in chapter 5.

As you look toward the next steps and building your frontline team, you first need to combine all the information discussed up to this point with your vision for the visitor experience. Chapter 6 will help you take this information and clarify your specific goals for service. Each museum is different, and you need to design a service model and an experience that is specific to your museum and your community.

The frontline team has the potential to make or break your visitor experience and is the key to your ability to meet your goals. Chapter 7 will help you clarify the roles of your team, and chapter 8 explores the possibility of blending the duties of security and service. Museums, including the Chrysler Museum of Art, have found success by combining these equally important tasks into one engaging role.

Once you are clear about who you are looking for, chapter 9 will help you select a vibrant and diverse team. You want to hire individuals with a great attitude knowing you can train the specific skills once they are on board. The heart of *Creating Great Visitor Experiences: A Guide for Museum Professionals* is in chapter 10 as you begin that training. You need to invest in the development of your team, and this development includes a rich onboarding training program and a commitment to ongoing education. There is always more to learn about your collection and exhibitions as well as about how to provide great service to your diverse audience. Your team needs to feel that they are valued members of the organization and they have support from all departments. Chapter 11 focuses on their morale by helping them feel connected to the institution.

To be truly successful, this visitor-centric philosophy and commitment needs to extend beyond the front line to create a true culture of service throughout your institution. The final chapter discusses how to accomplish this. Working together toward this goal will help you and your team realize your museum's ambitious mission.

# 1

## Focusing on the Visitor Experience

I love museums. I have loved museums since my first visit to the Museum of Science and Industry, Chicago when I was a child. I was fascinated when I could hear my friend speaking from across the room in the Whispering Gallery. I waited patiently for baby chickens to hatch right in front of me at the Baby Chick Hatchery. I ate delicious ice cream in *Yesterday's Main Street*, and I was mesmerized by the most amazing fairy castle I had ever seen. That fairy castle was created by silent-film star Colleen Moore, and I felt like I had some sort of special connection to her and the castle based on our shared first name. A book about that castle is one of the first souvenirs I remember seeing in a museum store. Everything in the museum seemed so exciting, and I couldn't wait to return.

Although I may see museums a little differently now that I have an insider's perspective, I still love visiting new museums of all kinds and returning repeatedly to my favorites. Apparently, I'm not alone. According to the American Alliance of Museums, nearly nine hundred million people visit museums each year.[1] Like those millions of others, I am not always looking for the same type of experience. Museums can be social, calming, and educational and can let you feel like a kid again. When I returned to that fairy castle as an adult, I'll admit, there were tears in my eyes. It's still a pretty magical sight.

Every museum has treasures that are meaningful to its visitors, and we don't always know which objects will resonate with each individual. Museums could choose to be vaults and to lock away all their treasures for safekeeping. However, the majority of museums are lively, active places that focus on connecting people to these objects. These museums truly believe that their experiences can enrich and transform lives.

The connection with those objects will be different for each visitor, and connecting the right experience to the right visitor is like solving a puzzle. I've always embraced this puzzle. I want to understand everything about each visitor, anticipate each visitor's needs, and wow them with an amazing experience. Ideally, I want to help connect all nine hundred million annual museum visitors to an amazing and personal museum experience.

## WHAT COULD BE GAINED FROM
## AN IMPROVED VISITOR EXPERIENCE

I've spent a lot of time talking with colleagues in the museum field, and it's clear when some-one doesn't believe in prioritizing the visitor experience. When you talk about improving cus-tomer service or being more thoughtful regarding your visitors, some people dismiss this as an attempt to be nice. They aren't vocally against the concept, but they don't believe that it is an intellectual pursuit or something that should rank highly on the institution's list of priorities. They believe these are soft or frivolous efforts and that museums are serious institutions with serious work to do. The condescension is clear in these situations, and more than once I've felt like someone wanted to pat me on the head as they used the word "nice."

Focusing on your visitor experience is not simply about creating a nicer environment, although I would argue that kindness is always important. It is about helping individuals con-nect to your collection. At its core, a great visitor experience helps you realize your mission. How do we make the environment comfortable so visitors are open to engaging and meaning-ful experiences? How do we make the items in our collection relatable to our visitors? How can our staff members engage with visitors in a way that enriches their visits? How do we welcome people who don't feel welcome in other public places? How do we recognize the differences among our visitors and adapt experiences to suit their preferences?

If you can answer these questions and improve your visitor experience, it can help you achieve several of your institutional goals. These goals may include growing and diversifying your audience, increasing your visitor satisfaction scores, or connecting to your community. The visitor experience impacts every visitor and can either cost you visitors or help you solidify and grow your audience.

## PEOPLE MAKE ALL THE DIFFERENCE

The largest influencing factor on the success of your visitor experience is the quality of your frontline team, and a successful frontline team doesn't form by chance. It requires careful selec-tion of the right individuals, thorough training, support from supervisors, and strong morale among the team. These individuals have the power to make or break the visitor experience. Unfortunately, they are not always given the training and support they need to shine.

There are some common misconceptions about all levels of service or hospitality staff. Some people believe that these jobs require no skills or expertise. It is true that, like in any other entry-level position, many people can step into a frontline service role and perform the basic functions. Some of the basic skills come simply from having been a customer and hav-ing the ability to picture oneself in the role of the visitor. There are people who meet the bare minimum and there are people who excel in this role, and the difference is profound. Many people can cook, but there is a wide range of skill level from a decent home cook to an all-star chef. You want a team of chefs.

The second-largest factor is the culture of service throughout your museum. The frontline team members, including the managers, don't have the power to create meaningful change without the support of the institution. They need other departments to believe in their goals, see them as colleagues, support their efforts, and put an emphasis on visitors. The visitor expe-rience will be best if all museum departments are focused on how their work impacts visitors.

**Figure 1.1.** *Source: Chrysler Museum of Art*

The gallery-host program at the Chrysler Museum of Art is successful because the gallery hosts are strong and talented individuals who are respected and supported by their managers and the museum as a whole. The museum has invested in this program, which blends security and service in the galleries. And the hosts are only one component of the visitor experience. Each department is focused on providing a strong visitor experience, broadening the museum audience, and engaging the local community. The gallery hosts open the door for each visitor, and this is a gesture of hospitality as well as a symbolic gesture. With the combined focus of the entire staff, the museum is trying to open doors and remove barriers for everyone.

## STRONG CONNECTIONS TO YOUR MUSEUM

We all spend a good portion of our time at home and work. However, there are additional places where we spend our time that are just as important to us, and these locations can be referred to as our "third places." This term was created by sociologist Ray Oldenburg and refers to places beyond work and home where people can have a good time, build relationships, and exchange ideas.[2] These places are community builders. They help us feel whole as individuals and help us connect to others who share our interests.

Our third place is unique to each of us. It may be the coffee shop we visit daily, our yoga studio, the church where we worship, the golf course, a favorite restaurant, or our local museum.

One of the groups that has the strongest connection to a museum is the dedicated volunteers that help fulfill the museum's mission. These volunteers could be your docents, who look forward to the training sessions from curatorial staff, gather for coffee with their fellow docents before leading their weekly school tours, gain fulfillment from presenting to the children on their tours, and stay for lunch at the museum after their job is done. They may also be frequent attendees of your evening member programs and some of your best customers in the museum store.

You may have other volunteers who gather weekly to arrange flowers for your public spaces or events, trustees who connect with fellow board or committee members, volunteers who help organize your donor events, greeters who help you welcome visitors, and volunteers who work in your museum store. For all these volunteers, your museum is an important part of their identities.

In addition to volunteers, you probably have regular visitors who know your museum well. These people may include visitors who gather regularly in the courtyard to discuss philosophy, finding the museum a fitting setting that showcases the history of humanity. They could be people who participate in studio classes regularly for a much needed creative outlet. They may feel so connected to the instructors that they bring donuts every time they take morning classes. Teenagers may visit every day after school to explore as well as to work on their homework in the courtyard until their parents pick them up. Visitors may come frequently to play the public piano. Women may hit the dance floor at every evening party. Parents of infants may visit the museum frequently to see other adults while they push their strollers through the galleries. Teachers may use your galleries as an extension of their classrooms, showcasing the museum in lessons of all kinds.

Not every visitor will see the museum as his or her third place, at least not initially. However, the idea of a third place showcases what museums can mean to their communities and the types of connections they can form. Even smaller connections can make a big impact.

## ONE SIZE DOES NOT FIT ALL

Museums are often reflections of their communities, and the visitor experience at each institution will reflect the museum's collection, visitors, and local community. Each museum is a unique institution, and what works in one location may fail miserably in another.

This can sometimes be a product of geography; what is considered friendly and welcoming in a small town may be off-putting and over the top in an urban environment. Museums that are located in cities with several other museums and experienced museumgoers may start their orientations differently from museums that see more novices. The content of your museum matters as well; what works in a science museum may not work in a history museum, even in the same city. The more you know about your museum, your community, and your visitors, the better prepared you are to offer outstanding service.

In addition to using my experience and examples from the Chrysler Museum of Art, I interviewed several museum hospitality professionals for this book. While we all tend to agree on large service concepts, there are many small differences in our approaches. Hopefully our experience can help you find your own voice when it comes to service.

I want to extend an immense thank-you to the following individuals for contributing to this project and for being strong colleagues over several years.

| | | |
|---|---|---|
| Ginny Fitzgerald | Chicago History Museum | Chicago, Illinois |
| Lauren Girard | Academy Museum of Motion Pictures | Los Angeles, California |
| Jeffrey King | Denver Art Museum | Denver, Colorado |
| Jessica Sharpe | Philadelphia Museum of Art | Philadelphia, Pennsylvania |
| Stacey Swanby | The Broad | Los Angeles, California |
| Janis Treiber | North Carolina Museum of Art | Raleigh, North Carolina |
| Stephanie Wood | Denver Museum of Nature and Science | Denver, Colorado |

## NOTES

1. "About Museums," American Alliance of Museums, https://www.aam-us.org/programs/about-museums/

2. "Third Places as Community Builders," Brookings, https://www.brookings.edu/blog/up-front/2016/09/14/third-places-as-community-builders/

# 2

## Understanding Museum Visitors
## and the Impact of the Visitor Experience

Despite the seeming popularity of museums, nearly nine hundred million annual visits as mentioned in chapter 1, museums are often trying to figure out how to attract a larger and more diverse audience. How do we attract those who aren't currently visiting? To make progress, we need to be true students of our field and gather all the information we can about museum visitors in general and about visitors to our institutions specifically.

### SOURCES OF INFORMATION

Information about museum visitors is available from a wide variety of sources, including national and local museum associations, independent researchers, and museum consultants. This research is valuable to all departments across the institution, and there are several portions of this research that are directly related to the visitor experience.

One engaging and useful source is Culture Track, an initiative of LaPlaca Cohen, a company that brands itself as a strategy and marketing firm for the creative sector.[1] Culture Track's research includes a national study of over 120 thousand cultural consumers in the United States. It focuses on the public's broadening view of culture and what people are looking for in a cultural experience. The information includes motivators and barriers, and it explores the complexity of visitors who are looking for more than one type of experience in a single visit. Beyond the visitor experience, Culture Track offers information about digital versus analog engagement, loyalty, and what motivates visitors to donate and support an institution.

The world is always changing, and so are people's attitudes and preferences toward museums. Particularly as the country emerges from a pandemic, no one is exactly sure how the future will compare to pre-pandemic habits. While we assume some things will be similar, it's important to always read the latest information from as many sources as you can. We know that some things will change, and if the pandemic has taught us anything, it's to expect the unexpected.

# TO VISIT OR NOT TO VISIT?

We all have many choices when it comes to our leisure time. On a Saturday afternoon, what captures your attention: a new movie at the theater, a local festival, or a museum exhibition? When traveling, where will you spend your time: touring a historic site, relaxing on the beach, or enjoying local cuisine? These are the choices that our visitors face, and understanding why they do or don't choose museums helps us create the right kinds of experiences for them.

## Why People Do Visit Museums

Do people visit museums because they want to learn something new, because they have an interest in the content, or because they want to experience new things? Those motivators are in the top five, but as you can see in figure 2.1, the top motivator is having fun.[2] That's very important for us to remember. We may see our museums as educational institutions, and this is absolutely the core of many museums' missions, but there is no reason we can't create experiences that are fun at the same time. This does not cheapen the experience; it enhances it.

The opportunity to feel less stressed also ranks highly on the list of motivators in figure 2.1, and this means something different to everyone. For some, it's simply the act of participating in an activity they enjoy. For others, it means an opportunity to reflect. What areas of your museum naturally allow for a peaceful or reflective experience? Make sure that these areas have ample seating, are comfortable, and allow for these experiences. Your team needs training to recognize these moments for visitors and allow visitors to have that introspective experience.

Feeling welcome is also listed as a popular motivator. This is directly related to a warm greeting and positive experience. The fact that this is ranked highly shows just how powerful your frontline team and creating a comfortable experience can be.

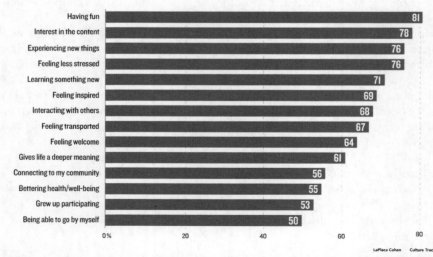

**Motivators For Cultural Participation**

| Motivator | Value |
| --- | --- |
| Having fun | 81 |
| Interest in the content | 78 |
| Experiencing new things | 76 |
| Feeling less stressed | 76 |
| Learning something new | 71 |
| Feeling inspired | 69 |
| Interacting with others | 68 |
| Feeling transported | 67 |
| Feeling welcome | 64 |
| Gives life a deeper meaning | 61 |
| Connecting to my community | 56 |
| Bettering health/well-being | 55 |
| Grew up participating | 53 |
| Being able to go by myself | 50 |

LaPlaca Cohen    Culture Track '17    32

**Figure 2.1.** *Source: "Top Line Deck Report," Culture Track '17 © Culture Track, LaPlaca Cohen*

While it's useful for us to categorize visitors in some ways based on their preferences, it's also important to remember just how complex people are. They are not always looking for one narrow type of experience, but sometimes they are looking for an exciting, varied one. With the visit motivators listed in figure 2.1, the research shows that 78 percent of those motivated to go alone also want to interact with others.[3] This may depend on the person's day or their companions, or they simply may need a few minutes alone during their visit.

Share this graphic with your frontline team. Can they recognize these motivations in your visitors? Can they give examples of times they have experienced these things at other museums? Taking it outside of your doors may help your team understand. Where in your museum do people feel most connected to their community? When have they felt inspired? You may want to have a few examples of your own ready in case the conversation stalls.

## Why People Don't Visit Museums

As shocking as it may be to those of us who love museums, some people genuinely have no interest in visiting cultural institutions. They simply prefer other activities. This may be because they have no interest in the content, or it may be because they don't think of museums when they plan their leisure time.

There are others who may consider going to museums but choose not to visit for reasons that are directly related to the visitor experience. In these cases, there are changes you can make inside your museum that can help you engage a broader audience.

### Museums Aren't for People Like Me

Because I spend a lot of time thinking about how to create a museum environment that is welcoming to everyone, it stings when I repeatedly see that one of the reasons people don't visit museums is because they don't feel that museums are for someone like them. This reason appears as the top barrier in the Culture Track report and has consistently ranked highly in several research studies over the years.[4] While this is a message we don't want to hear, it's one we need to listen to. These respondents may be telling us that they didn't feel welcome when they last visited a museum. It's also possible that they have never visited, but they believe that if they did, they would not be welcome. The reason why they feel this way may be very complex and based on socioeconomic factors, life experience, or influence from their friends and

**Barriers to Cultural Participation**

1. It's not for someone like me
2. I didn't think of it
3. It's inconvenient
4. I couldn't find anyone to go with
5. Its value is not worth the cost

LaPlaca Cohen    Culture Track '17

**Figure 2.2.   Source: "Top Line Deck Report,"**
**Culture Track '17 © Culture Track, LaPlaca Cohen**

family. No matter the reason for these feelings, creating a warm and welcoming experience for everyone should be a top priority as it can help us slowly change this mindset one person at a time. Be patient; changing this attitude is a long, slow process.

### Museums Are Inconvenient or Expensive

Inconvenience can mean something different for each institution. Is the museum far outside the city? Is traffic congested near the museum? Is parking limited? Are the hours limited? Do tickets need to be reserved in advance? While it's likely that not all these scenarios apply to your museum, you probably know which ones do. What are the challenges to visiting your museum? Are there ways you can remove these barriers or reduce their impacts?

The last-listed barrier is that the value is not worth the cost. This could indicate an admission fee that is too high, an experience that is lacking, or a combination of the two. In chapter 5, we'll discuss keeping an eye on the opinions of your visitors regarding your admission charge.

### Visitor Satisfaction or Dissatisfaction

Ninety-two percent of consumers say they trust the opinions of their friends and family above all other forms of advertising.[5] This can be a challenge for marketing since your institution can't control the message. What you can do is provide all your visitors with great experiences so the messages people share are positive.

The statistic above shows just how impactful one positive experience can be. For individuals who do not normally consider visiting, the opinions of their loved ones are much more valuable than anything you may say yourself. We also know that a negative message can travel faster than a positive one.

People cite previous negative experiences as a reason they are unlikely to visit museums. This is something everyone can relate to in a broader context. If you have a terrible experience at a restaurant, you are probably going to be reluctant to visit again. If you tried a new restaurant style or cuisine for the first time and had a bad experience, you may attach that view to all restaurants of that type. For example, if you visit a wood-fired-pizza restaurant for the first time and get a burned pizza and terrible service, you may assume you don't like wood-fired pizza and resist trying other similar restaurants. On the other hand, if you've enjoyed similar pizza in the past, you may let one bad experience roll off your back more easily.

In the same vein, frequent museum visitors may not consider one bad experience at a museum a big deal. It won't stop them from returning to that institution or visiting other museums. Negative experiences are going to weigh more heavily on the new visitors we are trying hard to impress. Beyond simply not returning to one museum, new visitors may associate a bad experience at one museum with all museums. With this in mind, we must consider ourselves ambassadors for all museums. The service we provide can have a large impact.

Some of the common negative experiences occur around the initial welcome as visitors arrive, the responses visitors get when they ask questions, and the enforcement of rules. We don't want to embarrass visitors or make them feel foolish. Creating positive experiences in these situations will be addressed in upcoming chapters.

### The Importance of Young Visitors

Frequent visitors are 39 percent more likely to participate in cultural activities because they grew up doing it.[6] This makes sense because the family experiences we have as children greatly influence how we spend our time as adults. When I was young, my father made sure I spent some memorable summer days at Wrigley Field, turning me into the eternal optimist, a loyal Chicago Cubs fan. Each winter, my mother and I took the train into Chicago to see productions of *A Christmas Carol,* influencing my love for live theater. My grandmother never missed an opportunity to dress in costume; her favorites were Donald Duck and Mrs. Claus. This created my love for costumes and lighthearted fun. When we traveled on a family vacation to Boston, we saw Paul Revere's house and Plymouth Rock, bringing to life the lessons in my history books. All these experiences helped form who I am and influenced how I spend my leisure time as an adult. We all have our own lists of childhood memories and family influences. We want our museums to be on these lists for our communities and visitors.

When people picture children in museums, they often see school groups touring with docents, learning in a unique way outside the classroom. The objects and displays in a museum can add a layer of understanding to students' lessons, and school visits can be a great introduction to museums. We should look for ways to connect with these students after their school visits.

See if you can send printed material either to the school or home with field-trip participants. This could be general information about the museum, information about upcoming family programming, or a discount coupon. Offering free admission for a future visit or a free or discounted membership to these students can encourage them to come back to the museum. If children ask their families if they can return to the museum, parents or grandparents may be likely to agree, even if it's not an activity they have participated in before. It's a joy for all of us to see young visitors sharing with their families what they learned on field trips. Some children can be seen lining up their families and taking on the role of docent as they share information. This adorable act could be the start of a new family tradition.

As families arrive at the museum, they will naturally look around for signs that children are welcome. There is a difference between feeling that the museum tolerates children as visitors and feeling that children are truly wanted. Consider the visual greeting people encounter as they enter your museum. Are children's guides, activities, and interactive play areas immediately visible, or are they hidden in the back? If they are not nearby, perhaps a colorful sign will convey the welcome message as visitors arrive.

You also want to be sure that children are welcomed during the greeting from your team. Are there family guides or activities your staff should offer? Do greeters have favorite areas or tips they could share with children? As families continue their visit, the staff should be welcoming to all members of the family. Ask questions to everyone equally, including the children in the party. Children love to share their opinions and favorites. When you are talking directly to children, get down to their level if possible. This sends a clear message that you want to hear from them. As you hire your frontline team, be sure that you have team members who excel at interacting with children. These staff members can help train their peers with engagement tips and techniques. These efforts will be very visible to children, and even more so to parents and grandparents.

*Engaging People of Color*

People of color are 82 percent more likely to stay away because activities don't reflect people from a range of backgrounds.[7] This staggering statistic demonstrates that museums need to be very conscious of what people see when they enter our institutions, both on the walls and with our staff. Are we showcasing all sides of the story? Are we featuring experts and artists of all backgrounds? When it comes to the visitor experience, is the frontline team diverse? Are they equally welcoming to everyone?

As mentioned above, people are more likely to visit museums as adults if they visited as children. While museums are currently making an effort to be more inclusive, that was not always the case. In fact, some museums were deliberately exclusive in the past. If museums were segregated or unwelcoming to someone's grandparents, it's unlikely those grandparents thought to take their children or grandchildren to museums. They found other leisure activities and created family traditions elsewhere. We should be conscious of what these individuals have been told by their families and be respectful of that history while we work hard to improve their impression of the museum.

You need to study the specific history of your museum and share the information with your team. Has everyone always been welcome? Was the museum or membership segregated? Were all groups allowed to use the museum for meetings or events? Has the content always represented varying perspectives? Understanding this history can help you understand some people's apprehension or mistrust. If you are dismissive of their experiences or argue with visitors about their perceptions, you are taking a large step backward.

Each experience is important, and we need to be very conscious of how our efforts are perceived by visitors of color and make sure each experience is the best it can be. We need to be understanding, patient, and genuinely warm and welcoming if we want to win over communities that we once did not include. This is a slow, but necessary and rewarding, process. As mentioned above, word of mouth is our most powerful marketing tool, and it can work for or against us.

There is some hope for future generations. The research of many museums shows that their young-adult visitors are their most diverse visitors in terms of ethnicity. It's a great sign that younger people of color feel comfortable visiting, and hopefully they can influence both older and future generations.

## The Importance of Accessibility

People with disabilities may have difficulty participating in leisure activities, and you want to be sure your museum is as easy to visit as possible. Each experience is important, as people with disabilities are 59 percent more likely to avoid traditional cultural activities because of a negative experience.[8] As mentioned above, word of mouth is important, and individuals with disabilities are likely to share their experiences, both positive and negative, with others in their community.

Being truly welcoming to individuals with disabilities goes far beyond meeting the minimum requirements stated in the Americans with Disabilities Act. This means really considering what would make the logistics of their visits easier so they can fully enjoy the experience. As will be discussed later, this might include offering large-print labels, ensuring that the museum is easy to navigate in a wheelchair, adding captions to videos, offering sensory-friendly hours, and offering ongoing training to your frontline team. This training is important as you want the team to feel comfortable welcoming individuals with disabilities. Your team should be able to offer assistance without being insulting or condescending and should act as an advocate for these visitors.

You want your staff to keep their eyes open and be thinking about how to make visitors more comfortable. For example, if they see someone struggling to stand while on a tour, you want them to find a way to offer the visitor a seat. If they notice that everyone in a wheelchair gets caught on a specific area of carpet, you want them to report it so it can be fixed. You should be open to suggestions for improvement, whether those ideas come directly from visitors or through your team. Look for opportunities to learn about your specific visitors and any challenges they encounter when visiting your museum. Doing this can help you create the best museum experience for your community.

## TYPES OF EXPERIENCES PEOPLE ARE LOOKING FOR

There is no one perfect experience for all visitors. People are unique and are looking for different things in a museum visit. The more we understand people's differences and desires, the better the experience we can provide each person.

When Culture Track asked survey respondents to choose the characteristics of an ideal cultural activity, the choices included options such as social, interactive, lively, hands on, active, calm, immersive, and reflective. As seen in figure 2.3, social and interactive activities appeared at the top of the list.[9]

Work with your frontline team and brainstorm what each of these characteristics might look like in your museum. If visitors are looking for social experiences, how could they have that type of experience in your institution? Are there exhibitions that encourage social activity, either with one of their companions or with a staff member? Do similar exhibitions also allow for interactive, lively, or hands-on experiences? Would you consider adding new exhibitions with these characteristics?

You should also consider which areas may offer a calm, immersive, or reflective experience. Once you identify these areas, how can you ensure they create the right environment for visitors who are seeking them? If people are looking for calmness in a specific area, is the area peaceful? Are there changes that could make the area more comfortable?

These exercises may help staff members recognize what visitors may be looking for in various areas of the museum. If your staff have identified that a specific area is good for lively or

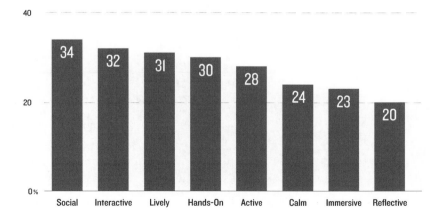

## Characteristics of an Ideal Cultural Activity

**Figure 2.3.**   *Source: "Top Line Deck Report," Culture Track '17 © Culture Track, LaPlaca Cohen*

social interactions, that area may be a great place to engage in conversation and ask questions. This may be very different from how your staff approach people in an area that is great for reflective experiences. Here they may take a step back and let visitors relax on their own unless visitors approach them and want to discuss the experience.

While figure 2.3 shows the top characteristics of cultural activities people seek, Culture Track found that these are not always distinct preferences but that there is overlap between characteristics. For example, of those who chose "calm," 15 percent also chose "active." Of those who chose "reflective," 24 percent also chose "social."[10] Again, this could vary from day to day, or people could want different experiences throughout their visit. This is why museums must offer a variety of experiences for people to enjoy.

While understanding these general traits helps you understand your visitors a bit more and likely comes from a level of research that few museums can afford, it is also important to focus on your unique visitors and learn more about them.

## NOTES

1. "What Is Culture Track?," LaPlaca Cohen, https://culturetrack.com/about-culture-track/what-is-culture-track/

2. "Top Line Deck Report," Culture Track '17, LaPlaca Cohen, slide 32, https://culturetrack.com/

3. Ibid., slide 58

4. Ibid., slide 41

5. "Consumer Trust in Online, Social and Mobile Advertising Grows," The Nielsen Company, https://www.nielsen.com/us/en/insights/article/2012/consumer-trust-in-online-social-and-mobile-advertising-grows/

6. "Top Line Deck Report," Culture Track '17, LaPlaca Cohen, slide 44, https://culturetrack.com/

7. Ibid., slide 46

8. Ibid., slide 45

9. Ibid., slide 51

10. Ibid., slides 51–53

# 3

## Learning about Your Museum's Visitors

Now that you've given some thought to museum visitors in general, it's time to examine your visitors and your community. Commit to learning as much as you can about your visitors and truly allowing their feedback to guide you. Each community is unique, and you want to tailor the best experience for your specific audience.

### WHAT DO YOU WANT TO KNOW, AND HOW WILL YOU USE THE INFORMATION?

The first step in learning about your visitors is deciding what information you want to know. What will help you understand your visitors more? What will help you work toward an improved visitor experience? Once you've collected this information, what will you do with it? Data collection doesn't have much value if you don't use the data to make adjustments and grow.

### Fundamentals of the Visit

Your questions about your visitors may start with what led visitors to your front door. Is this their first visit to the museum? What type of transportation did they use to get there? Do they live in the area or are they tourists? Who are they visiting with? Did they come for a specific program or exhibition? How did they learn about your museum? What motivated them to visit today? Understanding these pieces of information can help you provide a stronger visitor experience and then help you attract more similar visitors.

If you have a lot of first-time visitors, you need to recognize that you are constantly introducing your museum to new people, and that should be reflected in your visitor guide and your initial greeting and orientation. You want to share the highlights of your institution as people are just meeting your museum, and you want to give a well-rounded overview. If your visitors are mostly return visitors, you want to tell them what's new while allowing them to revisit their favorite exhibitions or works. They are the individuals who feel most connected to your institution, so you want to help them feel appreciated, and you want to look for opportunities that allow them to share their stories with others.

If you have a lot of out-of-town visitors, those individuals are also likely interested in the highlights of your collection. They may have limited time and want someone to help them plan the best visit. While you may feel you can't build a long-term relationship with these visitors, don't underestimate the power of great memories. Out-of-town visitors may take some great photos, share their visits on social media, and encourage others to visit. They can be some of your best ambassadors.

## Visitor Comfort and Movement

Once you understand the fundamentals of people's visits, you want to be sure you've met their basic comfort needs. Visitors can't have meaningful experiences if they are overheated, exhausted because there is nowhere to sit, or frustrated because they didn't understand your signs. Here you want to look at climate control, seating options, signage, and ease of navigating your museum and campus. For the most part, if you do these things right, you won't hear anything from your visitors. If you do these things wrong, you will hear about it, and hopefully you'll be willing to make changes.

The good news is you can act quickly on issues of visitor comfort. Visitors will often let you know, subtly or directly, when there is an issue. You do not need to wait until you collect a significant amount of data in this area; you can act on simple observations or comments. It's important to be alert to these concerns and listen beyond visitors' words.

Visitors may not specifically tell you that your signs are bad, but they may tell you that they couldn't find the parking lot and had to drive around the campus a few times. If visitors seem confused or lost in a particular spot inside the museum, examine your signage. For example, if people often ask for directions to the restroom when it is easily within sight, you should consider a different type of sign or different sign placement.

If additional seating is requested, see if you can rearrange your options or add additional choices. Ample seating that meets the needs of your visitors can result in longer visits and increased satisfaction and can prevent visitors from leaning on pedestals and walls. Consider a variety of options. If a bench won't fit, what about a few stools? Observe your visitors as they use your seating options. Do they struggle to stand up? Consider options with a greater height or with arms for support. Seating that works for all visitors will be discussed further in chapter 5.

Visitor comfort is largely influenced by the flow of visitors through your museum. How long do people stay at the museum? How do they travel through the building and campus? Where do they linger? Where do they breeze through? What do they skip? Are visitors with disabilities able to navigate the museum with ease? These questions are important to ask and will help you provide the best experience.

## Visitor Satisfaction

While museums track attendance, revenue, and other markers to determine success, one of the principal measures of success is visitor satisfaction. This marker helps you determine if your mission is truly accomplished. No matter how you choose to measure visitor satisfaction, it's one of the most important things to track.

Two popular metrics are the Net Promoter Score and the Overall Experience Rating.

# Net Promoter Score

On a scale of 0-10, how likely is it that you would recommend the museum to a friend or colleague?

| 0 | 1 | 2 | 3 | 4 | 5 | 6 | 7 | 8 | 9 | 10 |

Not at all Likely                                                                        Extremely Likely

|  | Sample Results 1 |  |  | Sample Results 2 |  |
|---|---|---|---|---|---|
| 0-6 | Detractors | 20% | 0-6 | Detractors | 15% |
| 7-8 | Passives | 50% | 7-8 | Passives | 30% |
| 9-10 | Promoters | 30% | 9-10 | Promoters | 55% |
|  | NPS = 10 |  |  | NPS = 40 |  |

**Figure 3.1.** *Courtesy of Author*

The Net Promoter Score was created by Bain & Company and is based on this question: "On a scale of 0–10, how likely are you to recommend XXX to a friend?"[1] The respondents are then broken down into three groups. Those who rate your museum 0–6 are your detractors, those who might share a negative experience or opinion with others. Those who rate your museum 9 or 10 are your promoters, those likely to share positive experiences or opinions. Lastly, those who rate your museum 7 or 8 are considered passively neutral and unlikely to share positive or negative opinions of your museum. We can all relate to this. Imagine a few stores or restaurants you have visited recently. Are there some you would give a low score and warn other people against? Some that were fantastic and you would highly recommend? And those in the middle that were just fine?

To determine your museum's Net Promoter Score, take the percentage of respondents who are promoters and subtract the percentage who are detractors. The final score will range from –100 (everyone is a detractor who rated your museum 0–6) to 100 (everyone is a promoter who rated your museum 9 or 10).

The Net Promoter Score is an excellent measure of visitor loyalty and overall affinity for your museum. This means it's a great tool to see how the community or your members feel about your institution as a whole. It may not be the right choice if you are looking at discrete experiences. For example, if you want to understand how people feel about a specific exhibition, there may be better tools. People may rate the exhibition highly because they are loyal to you and care about your institution even if that particular exhibition didn't meet their expectations.

The Overall Experience Rating is based on this question: "How would you rate your overall experience with XXX?" The choices are Poor, Fair, Good, Excellent, and Superior. This metric was created by the Smithsonian Institution and is based on the premise that we have a tendency to default to "excellent" when asked about our experiences.[2] "Excellent" becomes the baseline of an enjoyable experience. We expect that this will be the most common answer, and those who answer "superior" had a truly noteworthy time. Those who answer less than "excellent" had a negative experience. The Overall Experience Rating is a great way to measure a specific experience rather than the general opinion of your institution. If you use this question consistently, you will have a great metric to help you compare visits, programs, and exhibitions.

## Overall Experience Rating

How would you rate your overall experience with this exhibition?

- Poor
- Fair
- Good
- Excellent
- Superior

| Exhibition A | | Exhibition B | | Exhibition C | |
|---|---|---|---|---|---|
| Less than Excellent | 20% | Less than Excellent | 15% | Less than Excellent | 35% |
| Excellent | 50% | Excellent | 30% | Excellent | 40% |
| Superior | 30% | Superior | 55% | Superior | 25% |

|   |   |
|---|---|
| Less than Excellent | Superior |

**Figure 3.2.  *Courtesy of Author***

Whether you choose to measure visitor satisfaction with the Net Promoter Score, the Overall Experience Rating, a metric of your own design, or a combination of these tools, it's important to look at your scores over time. While it's useful to benchmark scores against other organizations, the most important measure can be comparing your institution's current and past scores. Hopefully, as you make changes in your museum, you will see positive changes in your scores. If scores drop, you can spot problems quickly so they can be addressed. Tracking scores can also show you the impact of various seasons, exhibitions, or programs. For example, you may see a dip when you bring on new team members because things are not yet running smoothly, and scores may increase during a popular exhibition.

It's important to break these scores down in multiple ways, and you may have to run several comparisons to find where there is a true difference. You could look to see if there is a score difference between visitors at various times of day, on certain days of the week, and during specific exhibitions. What is different about these times? You can also check to see if scores vary between locals and tourists. How are their expectations different? Are you meeting their expectations?

It's important to compare scores based on demographic data, such as household income, education level, age, and ethnicity. This can help you understand the different perspectives of your visitors. As you break down visitor satisfaction by demographics, you may learn about unintentional differences in your visitor experience. Did certain groups rate you lower? If so, you want to understand their reasoning as best you can.

You may run all the inquiries above, and while you may not see a significant difference among scores in many categories, you may notice a few variances. For example, you may notice that scores are higher on Tuesdays and Saturdays compared to other days of the week, and scores are lower with college students compared to other ages.

Once you note the differences, you then want to dig deeper to see if you can figure out the reason. The first step is to look at the abnormal scores and see if there are any comments on those surveys that help explain the variance. With the varying days of the week, you may find comments about a specific employee. Perhaps you have an absolutely stellar employee who works Tuesdays and Saturdays, and she has a large impact on the visitor experience. If someone is having that strong of an impact, you want to recognize her for that, and you may want her to lead a training for others so they can learn from her. You can also look at the profiles of visitors on those days and see if there are commonalities that may also contribute to the bump.

One museum did find that college students were consistently rating them lower than other age groups. Naturally, the staff wanted to dig in and figure out why. They looked at the surveys with the low rankings to see if they saw any comments that helped explain the scores. They also talked to the frontline team to see if they heard consistent feedback from this group. From both of those sources, they found that these students were very frustrated that they couldn't bring their backpacks into the museum. They also mentioned that they felt the staff was looking down on them, assuming they were going to break rules. They felt singled out and unwelcome based on these factors. The frontline team worked together to see how they could alleviate this. They adjusted how they talked about their backpack policy and worked on more positive engagement with these students in the galleries. After a few months, they saw an improvement in their scores with these students.

You can also use these scores to compare experiences over time. For example, if you ask your visitors to rate every exhibition using the Overall Experience Rating, you can compare each exhibition to the next. If you compare the Net Promoter Score based on zip code, you can determine where your loyal supporters live.

You can also parse out these exhibition scores by demographics. Which exhibitions were popular with families? with members? with people of color? with other target audiences you are trying to grow? If you are combining various data points, you may find that one exhibition had lower attendance but was extremely highly rated by those who attended. Depending on your goals, that may truly fit what you need. Ideally, you will set measurable goals at the beginning of an exhibition so you can be sure you're measuring what you really want to know and collecting the right data.

## Additional Opinions

There are likely additional questions you have for your visitors beyond visitor satisfaction. You can ask for specific feedback on dining options, the museum store, audio tours, drop-in programs, and any other element that is of interest to you.

Since staff and volunteers are such a key part of the visitor experience, it makes sense for them to be a part of your research. Many museums choose to ask if visitors felt welcome. This is a great indicator of both comfort and staff interaction. Others may use a sliding scale to rate the interaction with staff members. You may also want to separate distinct groups of staff, such as ticketing staff, tour guides, and store associates. If one group is shining above the others, you want to know why so you can spread the good behavior throughout the institution.

**Visitor Types or Personas**

As you collect more information about your visitors, you may discover that you can begin to group visitors into various categories based on their similarities. This isn't meant to pigeonhole them but rather create a tool that helps you facilitate better experiences for all your visitors. You are not saying that everyone will fit precisely into one of these categories, but understanding the differences between your visitors can help you begin to personalize the experience for each visitor.

This can be particularly useful to help staff members understand visitors who are very different from them. Many museum employees are avid museum visitors, which leads to the belief that they easily understand visitors' wants and needs. Unfortunately, museum professionals often do not represent the average visitor, and designing museums for only that group excludes huge portions of the community. Using visitor types or personas, you may begin to understand that visitors have different levels of loyalty to museums, preferences for engagement, comfort levels in museums, priorities during a visit, and patterns of visitation. Do they want to explore on their own or do they prefer a guided experience? Are they interested in staff interaction or a self-reflective experience? Are they museum experts or novices? Two of the Philadelphia Museum of Art's personas are "museum loyalist" and "experience seeker." These personas are understood across the institution and help departments communicate and create great visitor experiences.

Once these personas are developed, you'll want to utilize them in your staff training to help your team facilitate the best experiences for everyone. This training will be discussed further in chapter 10.

**Demographics**

It's important to collect demographic data from your visitors as part of an effort to be more inclusive. You need to understand how your visitors differ from your community as a whole, and these differences may showcase which groups aren't comfortable visiting your museum. It's useful for all museums to collect data on household income, age, ethnicity, education level, zip code, and number of children in the household. Beyond that, each museum should look at the community it serves to see what additional information it may want to collect. This might include how many visitors speak English as a second language, are active-duty military, or are recent immigrants. You are trying to build relationships with your specific community, and each community is different.

You want to compare your data to your local census data, which can help you put the information above into context. You may choose to compare your visitors to your city's or region's residents, or both, however you describe your primary audience. If your target audience is not your local community, you can apply this same concept to your city's tourists, school systems, or whoever you determine is your audience. Rather than using the census, you would use data from tourism bureaus or school systems as reference data.

Once you see where the differences are, you want to understand them. Are there barriers that are preventing visitation from certain groups? These barriers could be a variety of things and may take time to fully understand. Perhaps visitors from an underserved neighborhood can't reach you due to a lack of public transportation options. Families may not know if your museum is suitable for small children. Your admission fee may exclude those with a low household income. People of color may not have always felt welcome in your museum, and it may take generations to change that feeling. The best way to learn about these barriers and begin to remove them is to invest in relationships with underrepresented groups. These relationships will be discussed further in chapter 12.

## HOW WILL YOU COLLECT THE INFORMATION?

There are numerous ways to collect data about your visitors, and many are simple and inexpensive to implement. The information below is primarily focused on how you can collect information in-house, especially if you do not have a department or position specifically assigned to evaluation. For a larger investment, there are a number of wonderful national agencies that work with museums to facilitate formal observations, visitor studies, focus groups, and other research. You may also find great partnership with your local universities or museum associations. If those institutions are conducting larger studies, you may be able to join their projects, which can give you access to data you couldn't afford to collect on your own.

### Available Community Data

Yours is not the only organization that wants to understand its community. There is often a lot of data available through resources like the Chamber of Commerce, Economic Development Administration, and Census Bureau. Also, there are often great studies done by local media outlets, universities, and prominent businesses. If you have relationships with these institutions, they may be willing to share data with you. This is a chance to leverage your board of trustees, corporate members, and educational partners.

These organizations can report on demographic information, economic data, housing information, transportation in your area, and family composition. They may also have additional research on how people spend their leisure time. What activities do people enjoy? How much money do they spend? How do they learn about opportunities? How far in advance do they plan?

The information on how people spend their leisure time should be of particular interest to you and your marketing team. This will help you prioritize your likely limited marketing budget based on how far in advance people are planning their leisure activities and what resources they use to obtain information.

If there are activities that are popular with the same audience you want to reach, you should attend those activities and see what you can learn. Are there portions that could be adapted to your museum experience? In addition to duplicating those activities' strengths, you should see if there are ways for you to connect with people attending the activities. For example, you may be able to place a table at a local festival or have your executive director throw out the first pitch at a minor-league baseball game. You are reminding your audience of your museum's existence and showcasing its fun side.

### Ticketing Systems

Whether you are selling advance tickets online or simply greeting visitors as they arrive, the ticketing transaction is a great opportunity to learn about your visitors. The reports available on most systems can provide basic attendance information. What days and times are most popular? Do visitors come alone? Are they typically in groups of two, three, four, or more? When do members visit? What about families? This information allows you to plan programs and events at the best times for your visitors.

Many point-of-sale systems also allow you to ask additional questions as visitors enter. This is a great moment to capitalize on since you already have your visitors' attention, as long as you keep it brief. Some popular options include their zip codes, if they are first-time visitors, if they came for a specific program or exhibition, or how they heard about the museum. Choose what is most valuable to you as this is likely your data with the largest number of responses. You can vary the questions over time as your needs change. For example, if your goal for an exhibition is to connect to your local military community, you may want to add a question about military status for the run of that exhibition. If you are hoping to attract visitors from farther away during a particular season, you can collect zip codes during that time. If you are running a special marketing campaign, you can ask visitors if they've seen the promotion.

### Technology to Monitor Traffic Flow

Each year, new technology comes to the market that can help museums understand the paths their visitors take through their institutions.

People counters can be great to help you understand the traffic flow of your visitors. These have been around for a long time, and the technology becomes more advanced every year. Some use cameras that are very accurate and can identify the difference between adults and children. Placing these counters at key locations in your institution can help you understand how many people visit a particular exhibition or content area and how people move between spaces.

These counters will tell you if there is an area that doesn't get a lot of traffic, and from there you can do further studies to see if this is because the content is unpopular or because the area is hard to find. If it's the latter, additional signage or mention in your visitor guide may help. If the content is not of interest, is there a way you can help your visitors connect to this material? You could add a video or a hands-on activity, change how you talk about the exhibition, or provide additional training for the frontline staff. If there are multiple entrances to a gallery, people counters could tell you how people are entering and exiting that room. This may not be what you expected. Once you know which doors people are using, you can ask yourself if your signage is in the right location. If people are moving in unexpected ways, you may need to move or duplicate signage.

If you don't have people counters, you may be able to use your security cameras to answer some of your questions. You can watch for a period of time to see which doors are used or where people linger. This is a much more tedious method, so you would only use it to answer very narrow questions.

### Surveys

There are infinite possibilities when it comes to surveys, and most museums are utilizing at least one kind in their work. Here we are specifically focused on surveys related to casual visitors rather than programs or tours.

A popular on-site option is an intercept or exit survey. These are used by picking a point in the museum, whether the exit or another key location, and approaching every third (or a number of your choosing) person who crosses the point. This offers you the best statistically random sample and is hopefully an accurate cross section of your visitors with statistics you can rely on. It's important to make sure you vary as many factors as possible. If you survey only on Sundays, you'll miss the young families who come on weekday mornings. If you survey only in the summer, you are likely to miss the seasonal visitors you may only see in the fall or winter. As you set up your plan, be sure to look at the time of day, day of week, season, and survey collectors themselves. Plan for as much variety as possible to get the best results.

You also can email a survey to visitors after their visit. If a visitor purchases their ticket on-line, you already have their email address. You can also collect email addresses during transactions at your admission desk and in your museum store. Visitors will have more time to fill out surveys at home, so you can ask for a little more of their time. But if your survey is too long, you're likely to frustrate your visitors. They may not finish the survey, and this may impact their overall opinion of you. The Philadelphia Museum of Art has used a "Tell Us" survey for over ten years that is based on visitors' experiences and asks questions about the welcome visitors received, the admission process, the retail experience, and more.

Also, be sure that visitors can easily skip the email request in the museum. You don't want to negatively impact their visits, especially during the process of trying to learn more about your visitors and offer them better service. Some people don't want to share this information, and that should be respected.

If these options sound complicated, you can start with a simple comment card or a touch screen with only one question on it. The North Carolina Museum of Art utilizes a comment card with three questions, including what they consider the most important: "Did you feel welcome?" This feedback has helped shape the institution's campus host program and its staff training.

## Listening to the Front Line

Frontline staff can be a conduit to bring feedback from visitors to the rest of the museum staff. They have a lot of knowledge about your visitors, and it's important to be sure they have a way to communicate with others in the museum.

Some of this knowledge comes from observing visitors. Frontline staff know where visitors most often get lost. They also know the frequently asked questions in each area, what visitors find confusing, what attracts children the most, and where visitors most frequently break the rules. A curator may not know how popular an object is with children, and the information from the frontline staff may prevent curators from placing the object too high. The person who writes the labels may think a term is common vocabulary for everyone, but the staff may know that people frequently ask for the definition. These items are easy to correct and can help future visitors have a stronger experience.

Frontline staff also overhear casual comments from visitors: "That wasn't as good as last time." "I thought this exhibition was about something different." "I wish there had been a warning that this exhibition included animal cruelty." These are all very important pieces of feedback to consider, even if they weren't written on a survey or even communicated directly to staff.

Often visitors will make casual comments to staff that they may not want to tell a supervisor or write down in a survey. The candid reactions like the overheard comments above are important. You should find a way to collect this rich feedback from the frontline staff and look for commonalities. You can have staff members submit these via email or write them on feedback cards, and one employee can be responsible for organizing this information and looking for ways to share it throughout the institution. If you hear the same thing repeatedly, you need to make a change.

Learning about your visitors, including the creation of visitor types or personas, can help you as you train your frontline staff and will be discussed in chapter 10. As you learn more, the training will evolve, and the visitor experience will continue to improve.

Now that you have collected this information and begun your evaluation, we will look at how you can map the path of your visitors and identify the key moments in your visitors' journey.

## NOTES

1. "Measuring Your Net Promoter Score," Bain and Company, https://www.netpromotersystem.com/about/measuring-your-net-promoter-score/

2. "Visitor Experience," Smithsonian Public Engagement Dashboard, https://www.si.edu/dashboard/public-engagement

# 4

## Visitor Mapping

### Charting Visitor Routes through Your Institution

Understanding how your visitors move through your institution can help you in your quest to improve the visitor experience. The journey-mapping process helps you create a graphic representation of the way visitors flow through your museum. This is a useful way to share information with new employees, trustees, or volunteers. This is more than just interesting information; it is a tool that helps you improve the experience by considering each step along the way, working to lessen the negative moments and enhance the positive ones.

This chapter largely focuses on an exercise that will help you create a map, or multiple maps, to show this journey.

#### DECIDING WHO GETS A SEAT AT THE TABLE

As with all brainstorming and group-work activities, having the right people at the table is the key to success. This is a great opportunity for staff members from various departments to work together on a joint task and form relationships that will serve them well beyond this project.

It's essential that you have frontline staff involved in this process and that you choose the right representatives from the group. The delegates need to be able to see the larger picture of the visitor experience outside of their individual roles, have a high level of empathy for visitors, and be comfortable speaking up with colleagues at all levels of the organization.

These individuals may not necessarily be your top performers or most experienced employees. Some people are excellent in their roles but struggle to see beyond their own performances. They see only the visitors they are interacting with at that moment. Others may be very naturally empathetic toward visitors but have trouble articulating the thoughts behind their actions. When asked to explain how they read visitors and know how to respond in a way that each visitor would prefer, they may not be able to put it into words. They may reply that they simply just do it. These skills make them excellent fits for their jobs but bad matches for this activity.

Since this group will include representatives from all areas of the organization, you need to choose frontline team members who are comfortable participating and speaking up in that environment. Some excellent team members and supervisors have great opinions but find that situation uncomfortable. Choose those who will contribute to the discussion.

You should also include people beyond the frontline team members who understand the experiences of your visitors. These could include educators, senior staff members, and managers and supervisors from all forward-facing departments, such as security, the museum store, or food service.

### Guiding the Conversation

Additionally, you will need to choose someone to lead the exercise who can listen to all opinions, keep the conversation moving, design a plan for the exercise with multiple approaches, and work to form a consensus. This person may be someone from the outside who isn't as invested in the content and doesn't have any preexisting opinions about your visitors. If that isn't the right fit for you, choose a staff member who has the same qualities. The person could be someone from another department disconnected from the visitor experience who would otherwise not be involved in this process. It could also be the leader of your visitor experience team.

The person you choose to facilitate this process will need to plan ahead and have questions in mind if the conversation stalls. It can be useful to read reviews from visitors in preparation. Trends will probably be visible. What do visitors love? Where are there frustrations? If these ideas don't come up naturally in the conversation, the facilitator will need to present them.

The facilitator also needs to create an environment in which people are comfortable collaborating. Depending on the size of your group, everyone may want to divide into smaller groups, where people are more talkative. In this case, give each small group a portion of the exercise to brainstorm, or have each group work on the same portion at once and then come back together for discussion.

## MAPPING THE VISITOR JOURNEY

Throughout this exercise, you will mentally walk through the experience of your visitors. You will note each step or idea on a sticky note, then arrange the sticky notes in the right order as you move forward. You may need to insert new notes in the journey, group notes together, or remove notes as you proceed. The sticky notes provide an easy way to move ideas around throughout the process.

### Planning Their Visit

The true beginning of a museum visit occurs long before a visitor walks through your doors. What is a visitor's first introduction to your museum—an advertisement, a story from a friend, a social media post? Once interested, how does the visitor learn more—stories from friends, your website, a phone call? You'll need to consider all the ways people learn about your institution and how they plan their visits so you can gather as much information as possible.

Start by making a list of the ways visitors are introduced to your museum. This list will be unique to your community and museum. If you welcome a lot of tourists, those people may find your museum through a local tourism bureau, a travel website, or a recommendation from the front desk of a hotel. If you are in a college town, students may be sent to your museum to complete assignments. Do you have a frequent off-site presence at local festivals or events where people may discover you? Brainstorm these options as well as the types of social media, advertising, and public relations channels you frequently use. You may be able to gather this information from survey data, website analytics, or anecdotal experiences from the frontline team. If the list of sources is long, you may want to narrow it to your top five or ten.

Once you know how visitors first hear about your museum, create a list of ways they research details. In some cases, there may not be an additional step after the introduction above. The hotel employee may mention your museum and tell visitors details such as the hours, prices, location, and current exhibitions. Other visitors may take casual recommendations from people they know and get the detailed information from your website, through a phone call to your institution, or through a search engine. Make a second list of these information sources.

Are there additional steps before someone visits your museum, such as reserving tickets for admission, special tours, classes, or experiences? If these decisions and transactions need to occur before your visitors are on-site, be sure to include them in a step on your journey map.

These first steps might read INITIAL INTEREST → RESEARCH → TICKET PURCHASE.

### Warm Welcome

The core of your journey map will show what happens after people have made the decision to visit your museum and they arrive on your campus.

Begin by considering how visitors travel to your museum. Do most visitors drive? If so, is there ample and easy-to-find parking? Are directions to parking areas and prices clearly posted? Do visitors arrive via public transportation? Are the routes from local stops marked clearly via signage and on your website? Are you in an urban center where visitors may walk by and spontaneously decide to visit? If so, do those visitors understand what your museum is from the building's exterior?

Once visitors arrive on campus, be sure they can easily find the building's entrance. This may sound like a small item, but it can make a big impact. Remember that some visitors are apprehensive and anxious. We know that one of the top reasons people don't visit museums is that they don't feel museums are places for people like them. If they are unsure if they are at the right door, this small concern can exacerbate their feelings.

At many museums, the first staff interaction is at the main entrance. This may be a security presence to check bags and monitor entry, or it may be a welcoming greeting. This interaction may need to accomplish both tasks, and both are equally important. What is this greeting like at your museum?

Once through the door, many visitors make their first stop at an admission or ticketing desk. Even museums that offer free admission often want visitors to check in so they can get an accurate attendance count, collect some information, and offer a welcome and orientation. You may already have an outline for the transaction process at your admission desk; if so, you can add those steps to your journey map. If you do not have this process written out, now is an opportunity to do so. The interaction at the admission desk is a key moment, so be sure you have accounted for each step, including the greeting, ticketing process, possible membership pitch, additional experiences, orientation, and sharing of key information such as policies or daily events.

These steps might be on your map labeled as ARRIVAL ON CAMPUS → PARKING → MAIN ENTRANCE → TICKETING.

## Galleries and Exhibitions

The heart of a museum visit is the exploratory voyage through the unique exhibitions and galleries of an institution. Some museums are structured as linear or one-way experiences that guide visitors on a specific path through the institution. Others are designed for visitors to explore in multiple directions of their own choosing.

Consider the common routes through your museum. If there aren't any, you may want to consider breaking routes down by section, wing, or exhibition. Are there common routes through those areas? If there is at least one area that has a general traffic pattern, start with that area as you get into the exercise. Mentally walk through each area and note your route. If your group struggles with this exercise, you may want to take them into the galleries and physically walk through. That can sometimes help you accurately record the path.

If you have an area that includes challenging content, something emotional or controversial, consider where in the journey visitors encounter that content. What will visitors see right before or after? People are more open to this content in the right context. Ask yourself if there is a natural buildup to and recovery from this content. Some museums have found that people are more open-minded and receptive to this type of content later in their museum visits and have more negative reactions when the material is placed closer to the entrance or near material that is very dissimilar. When material feels out of place to visitors, their perception of the content is impacted.

## Amenities

Visitors consider your amenities, such as a restaurant, museum store, theater, or demonstration area, as important components of their visits, and you need to consider them as you work on your journey map.

If people come for the restaurant or museum store specifically, you may want to consider the journeys of those visitors. Can they go directly to those destinations? Do they have to wait in a long line? Do they still have to pay admission? What is the visit like after their meal or shopping excursion? If people usually visit these amenities only as part of the larger visit, the journey map may be different, but you still want to include these amenities on it.

If you have multiple dining options, you should consider if the decision-making is clear to your visitors. Can they tell the difference between your fine-dining and casual options? Are menus readily available? Be sure this information is easy to obtain and understand.

The museum store is frequently the final stop of a visit, but that may not be true of all museums. Wherever the store falls in the journey, you need to include it on the map. If your store is large or complex, you may want to map the route inside the store or the steps involved in a transaction.

If there are other amenities or attractions in your museum, such as an optional theater, hands-on activity, or demonstration, you need to include them on your map as well.

## Post-visit

Once you've thought about the journey through your museum, consider what happens after the visit. Visitors may have the perfect treasure from the museum store in their homes, they've shared their photos on social media, and they are ready to share their stories with friends and family. Do you encourage them to share their visits in these ways? If you collected their contact information, do you reach out to them to offer a survey or encourage future visitation? Take a moment to note any portions of the post-visit that are important to your visitors' journey.

## MOMENTS OF TRUTH

All portions of the visitor experience are not created equal. Some moments have the potential to influence visitor satisfaction more than others. Once you've walked through the entire experience, take some extra time to identify these key moments.

You can overlay these key moments on your journey map, perhaps by adding a colored dot to the corresponding sticky notes. You can also map key moments independently. If your group is struggling with the mapping exercise, key moments may be an easier place to start. You can talk about the moments that make the biggest impacts. For many people, the negative items are easier to identify than the positive, so asking about the pain points can be a great way to start the conversation.

### Pain Points

Even your favorite experiences have their low points. People who love to travel may find going through airport security to be a frustrating chore. It can be a lot of fun to cheer on your favorite football team at a live game, but few people enjoy the traffic jam as they exit. The overall enjoyment of an activity must be large enough to outweigh the difficult moments.

Consider the journey that you mapped above. Where are the potential pain points in a visit to your museum? These will be unique to your institution, and you must be aware of them. You can begin by reading your online reviews and talking to the frontline staff about common complaints.

Some pain points may exist before people arrive at your door. For example, perhaps traffic in your city is terrible and you know visitors will arrive at your institution frustrated. They could also be frustrated if your on-site parking is limited, confusing, or expensive. Perhaps after all those battles, they encounter long lines to enter your institution or an admission charge that is a surprise to them.

If you are missing expected amenities, that can be frustrating for your visitors. These amenities include ample restrooms, water fountains, food and beverage options, an exciting museum store, easy-to-understand signs, and plentiful and comfortable seating. It's also possible that these amenities may exist but may not be in the right locations or may not meet the expectations of your visitors.

In the same vein, people may be frustrated or disappointed with your offerings regarding accessibility. This goes beyond building structure and can include program offerings, staff interaction, or easy-to-correct items such as a lack of captioning in a video or not offering a visitor guide in large print.

If you have signature objects or exhibitions, do they live up to expectations? Are these areas crowded, or do people often walk away disappointed? We've all seen museums where people swarm around one object, and many people feel let down once they see the object in person. If this is true of your museum, it's important to note.

For most institutions, security is a necessity to protect the collection and for the safety of staff and visitors. However, interactions with security are also reported to be pain points at some institutions. This includes security checks at the entrance, rule enforcement in the galleries, and

an intimidating presence that makes some visitors uncomfortable. These interactions are necessary, but how the message is delivered is important. Options for blending security and service
are discussed in more detail in chapter 8.

In addition to security interactions, all other staff interactions need to be considered. What
are the visitor perceptions of your team? Is your staff always welcoming? Where are there areas
for improvement?

As mentioned earlier, a previous negative experience is one of the top reasons people don't
visit museums. Sometimes an experience is negative because employees assume visitors understand museum operations when they don't. This could include officers at the door assuming
visitors know they need to have their bags inspected. Officers may stand staring and waiting
for visitors to open their bags without giving a friendly greeting and instruction. It could also
be staff members using insider terminology or assuming visitors know museum rules. These
practices can be alienating for visitors, which reinforces another top reason people don't visit
museums: they don't believe museums are for people like them. Explaining security practices
or terminology isn't dumbing things down as sometimes referred to in the museum field; it's
bringing everyone to a level playing field. Once everyone is in the same place, they can have
great experiences and feel like they belong. Take this time to know where visitors could feel
like outsiders in your museum, and then work on fixing it.

A negative experience could also come from poor service. This could be a negative tone
of voice or body language, a condescending attitude, or a lack of interaction and ignoring
visitors. It could also be a lack of recognition of when visitors would like to explore on their
own and would prefer less staff interaction. How do visitors respond to your service at various
points in their visits? Where are the weak points and opportunities for improvement?

As you identify, and hopefully alleviate, the pain points in your visitor experience, it helps
to pay attention to the complaints you hear from visitors. For example, if people are complain-
ing about a hard sales pitch from your team, you know that is an area you need to improve.
How can you accomplish your goals in a way that is more palatable to your visitors? Like in
all other areas, keep your ears and your mind open.

## Opportunities to Wow

On the opposite end of the spectrum from the pain points are opportunities to surprise and
delight your visitors. Perhaps there is an installation in your entryway that always brings a
smile, a popular object or exhibition, or something your staff does that is always a big hit.
Review any exit surveys you have conducted to see what is mentioned as visitor favorites.

All museums can find opportunities to wow their visitors during interactions with frontline
staff. This can include a small gesture such as taking a photograph of a group or carrying a
heavy item to a visitor's car. It could be helping someone with a disability find a way to enjoy
the museum more easily. A tour guide who offers great information and makes learning fun
could wow an entire family.

These moments can also include surprising opportunities to interact with your content,
such as a touch tank at an aquarium, a chance to play a replica of a historical instrument, or a
behind-the-scenes tour. These types of experiences can easily be the highlight of a visit. Make
a list of favorite experiences and moments so you know where the opportunities are to delight
your visitors. Where are there additional opportunities?

## PULLING IT ALL TOGETHER AND CREATING A MAP

At this moment in the exercise, you likely have a table or wall full of sticky notes. While the act of the exercise alone can be beneficial, in order to make it as useful as possible for your team, you will need to showcase the information in an easy-to-understand graphic diagram or map. What should this map look like? Maps will vary by museum, and even a very basic diagram like figure 4.1 will be useful. If it's possible for you to work with a graphic designer, the map project will greatly benefit from their expertise.

Depending on the drafts and lists you've created with your sticky notes, you may need to edit or condense some of the work you've done. You may want to group similar items or choose only the most popular options in order to make the map easy to read. This can also be a good opportunity for you to show your notes to a larger group than just those who helped in the map's development. You may gain additional insight as more people are able to participate.

Your museum may encourage visitors to follow a linear path. In this case, your map may look like the exhibition map in figure 4.2. Such a map can help your team see how the visit progresses and evolves through an exhibition or the entire museum.

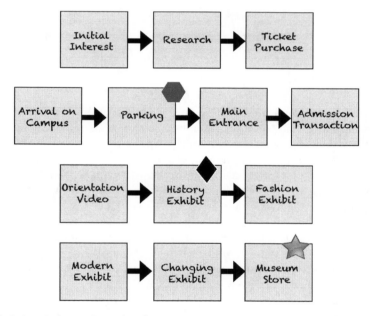

 Pain Point - Parking is limited and expensive. Visitors are frequently frustrated.

 Potentially Challenging Material - The History Exhibit features information about the enslaved servants of the area. Staff members need to be comfortable discussing this information.

 Opportunity for Wow - The Museum Store is one of the best in the city and has a reputation for excellent customer service.

**Figure 4.1.** *Courtesy of Author*

# Curly Hair History Exhibit

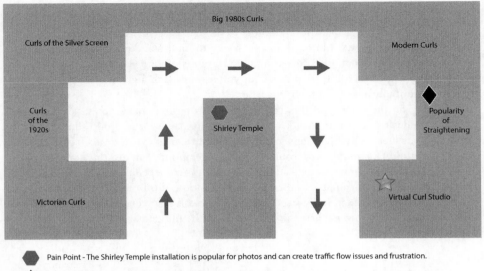

Pain Point - The Shirley Temple installation is popular for photos and can create traffic flow issues and frustration.

Potentially Challenging Material - Some people feel this doesn't belong here. Staff should be prepared to discuss.

Opportunity for Wow - This interactive is popular, especially when the staff members offer instruction and take visitor photos.

**Figure 4.2.** *Courtesy of Author*

In another example, a museum may have three distinct experiences: a historic home, an expansive garden, and an outdoor kitchen. You may determine that your visitors are likely to visit all three, but the order varies between visitors. However, within each of the three areas, there is a predictable pattern. If that is the case, your map may have three separate circles, one for each area, and people move between the three at their own pace. Your efforts should be spent understanding the experience within each attraction rather than trying to figure out in which order people visit the three attractions.

You may discover that you need to create a few versions of your journey map. Families may follow a much different pattern from adult visitors, so you'll want a graphic that shows each option. You may also want to break down the differences among the visitor personas you have developed. You don't need too many versions of your map, but if there are large differences between routes, you should create a few variations.

## MAKING YOUR MAP A USEFUL TOOL

The purpose of this exercise is not simply to create a graphic that shows how visitors move through your museum. The goal is to better understand your visitors, and this graphic will be one tool to help you as you continually work to improve your visitor experience. Once the graphic is complete, you can work to develop and improve every step along the journey.

You began by identifying the most common ways people hear about your museum. Do those sources have access to the best information? For example, do local hotel employees know what your museum is and consider it a top destination to share with their visitors? If you determine that hotel employees may not know your institution as well as you would like, what can you do about that? Can you invite them to visit or offer free admission passes? If hotel employees are a primary source of information for your visitors, you may want to invest in a breakfast or after-hours event for tourism staff. If hotels are a less popular source of information but still common enough to make your list, perhaps you can simply drop off some brochures and a list of frequently asked questions. If social media is a primary source of information, you may want to increase your investment in that area. Do you have a staff member dedicated to social media? Do you post content frequently? Engage in this discussion for each item on your list.

You took the time to identify key moments in the visit, both positive and negative, so you can work to either improve the experience in the negative areas or maximize the positive impacts of popular aspects of your museum.

For each of the pain points, groups can brainstorm solutions to the problem. You want to correct as many issues as possible, but unfortunately, some problems do not have a simple solution. You have limited power over outside stressors such as traffic or weather. Even in cases where you cannot completely fix a problem, there are often things you can do to mitigate the situation. You can't change the hot weather, but you can offer cooling stations and loaner wheelchairs in outdoor areas.

If people are upset that your historic home is not wheelchair accessible, you may not be able to do major renovations to the historic property, but perhaps there is a way to add ramps in some areas without damaging the integrity of the home. You can also look for opportunities to allow visitors to see inaccessible areas of the house through a virtual tour.

You will also discover things that are totally within your control. You can offer staff training to help alleviate pain points or to help the team understand the opportunities to wow. You can also change some of the structure of your staff interactions, such as the greeting or the positioning of staff. The staff members are an important component of the visitor journey and an area where you should dedicate your energy.

If a popular item doesn't live up to expectations, you certainly don't want to remove it, but examine how you are using the object in marketing. Perhaps positioning it differently will lead to less disappointment. You also can try to increase your use of other objects to cultivate new favorites.

As you lead discussions with your team about these pain points, don't be afraid of challenging questions. Are the pain points the same for everyone, or do they read differently to historically underrepresented groups? For example, if people are reporting that the greeting at the door is unwelcoming, it's important to dig in and see if it's unwelcoming for everyone or if those comments come more from families or people of color. You want to make sure you understand the real concerns, even if they are hard to hear, so you can address them.

Creating this journey map has helped you visualize the paths that visitors follow through your institution. The next step is to set up your museum to welcome visitors.

# 5

## Start with the Basics

### Making the Museum Itself Welcoming

The frontline team has a tremendous impact on the visitor experience, and subsequent chapters of this book will thoroughly discuss how to optimize this team. However, this chapter focuses on setting the museum building or campus itself up for success and facilitating a great experience. Each museum has several decisions to make about general operations, including operating hours, styles of visits offered, admission fees, visitor policies, and amenities. These decisions are guided by staffing logistics, budgetary needs, and staff preferences, but the needs and preferences of your visitors should be front and center.

#### HOURS AND ADMISSION

When people are interested in visiting your museum, the first pieces of information they will look for is your hours and the admission price. These items may have remained unchanged for a long time, but it is worth a moment of consideration to see if they are helping you serve your visitors in an optimal way. Your hours and price may be the best they can be, but you should reevaluate from time to time as your audience evolves.

#### Operating Hours

Your posted hours of operation represent your invitation to your visitors, and that invitation will rightly vary by institution. If you understand your existing visitors as well as others in your community who you would like to attract, you can determine the best hours for your institution. Most museums are trying to balance the needs of diverse visitors with the needs of the institution. Be sure the visitors are at the forefront of this discussion and you are not solely focused on longtime policies or what is easy for your institution.

You should begin by learning about the preferences of your existing visitors and your target audiences. You may discover that young families prefer early-morning hours before nap time. Young professionals may like evening hours when they can relax with friends. Retirees may want to leave by early afternoon in order to avoid rush-hour traffic.

You should also look at the unique patterns of your community. If there are major employers in the area, you should understand those employees' work patterns because they will impact many local families. If you are on a college campus, commuter students may want to visit on weekdays when they are on campus for classes while residential students may like to visit in the evenings for date nights. If you are near a tourist destination or convention center, you may want to understand the flow of those travelers to determine when they may like to visit. Is there a large after-church crowd? There is no one right answer that suits all museums or all members of your community. You need to choose the hours that work for your visitors specifically.

Although your visitors should be front and center as you choose your hours, there are operational concerns that also impact these choices. You may need to leave many weekend evenings available for revenue-generating rental events. Depending on the layout of your museum, you may also need at least one closed day per week for exhibition installation or maintenance. These needs certainly impact your hours, but make sure they are genuine needs and not just the way things have always been done.

You may also be limited by budget. Each hour that you are open has associated costs, including salaries of the frontline team (including workers in security, visitor services, and the museum store), increased utility usage, and needs from the facilities team. You can determine the number of staff hours you can afford and then choose the best way to allocate those hours. You may have to make hard choices about extending evening or morning hours or being open more days per week.

There are a few ways to identify slow hours that you could eliminate if necessary. Your first resource is the frontline team because they spend each day observing your visitors and can tell you about visitation patterns. Of course, some team members will be better about documenting these observations than others. You can also use electronic people counters to track visitors entering and exiting the building and use those time stamps to understand the ebb and flow of attendance. If an electronic people counter is out of your budget, you can have a staff member near the entrance use a clicker that adds and subtracts visitors. Either solution allows you to know how many people are in your museum at any given time. If you are trying to evaluate past attendance patterns from before you used these procedures, combine the average visit length with the admission times in your point-of-sale system.

It's a bit more difficult to determine which hours would be busy if you added them. Ask your security team to check the cameras at the main entrance or in the parking lot. Are there consistently people trying to visit at times when your museum is closed? Is there a crowd waiting when you open for the day? You also can talk to staff who answer the museum's telephones. They have insight based on the questions they hear visitors ask. You should utilize surveys and focus groups to determine potential hours, but be aware that sometimes there is a difference between the hours visitors say they want and the times they will actually attend. They may overestimate what they will be able to do. You should still engage in this conversation, but you may want to try opening during new hours on a trial basis before committing to a change.

You can use occasional or seasonal hours to test these different options on a trial basis or to fulfill a need that you can't meet consistently. For example, it may not be possible to hold evening hours every week, but perhaps you can offer one evening per month. You also may decide to try extended hours for the summer to see if they are popular. You could open early on select weekend mornings and change the experience to be more sensory friendly.

You also can use programming to fulfill visitors' needs. One of the most popular options is an evening event with music and drinks that draws younger crowds and is focused on growing the museum audience. You also may choose to offer something like periodic wine-pairing dinners instead of having your restaurant open every evening.

There also may be times when you consider opening your museum for holidays. There are visitors looking for family-friendly activities on some holidays, and museums could be that special destination. You need to be cautious as you consider this and will need to balance holiday hours with allowing as many of your employees as possible to be home with their own families. Do not add holiday hours unless you are relatively sure you will be successful. It's demoralizing to work on a holiday when there isn't anyone to serve.

If you decide to open on holidays, you need to be transparent with your frontline staff, give as much notice as possible, offer additional compensation, provide a meal, and say a genuine thank you. Members of the leadership team should visit the museum to say thank you in person and assist with crowds. Whether you open or not, there will always be a security team that has to work on these days. These staff members often take pride in their responsibility, and they deserve all the benefits listed above. It's important to recognize them for their work.

## Pricing

The experience of visiting a museum is priceless, but practicalities require that many museums charge an admission fee.

You need to keep an eye on how your admission price is perceived. If you charge general admission or admission to special exhibitions, you should include a question about value on your general survey. While you are unlikely to have everyone tell you that your admission is too low, you should watch to see if people feel strongly that the museum is not a good value for the admission cost. If this is persistent feedback and your attendance is lower than you would like, you may want to consider lowering the fee. You should also watch how perceptions change over time. This lets you know if you could increase your admission fee as necessary or if your audience is changing. New visitors may feel differently from your established visitors. You can keep an eye on your visitor feedback also, whether those comments come online, in person, or through your frontline team. Are people surprised about the fee or do they complain about it? Do these comments come usually from first-time visitors or returning visitors? Do the comments come from families? This information will help you move forward.

If you have the flexibility to offer discounts, you can use this to reach your target audiences. For example, if you are trying to attract families, you can offer discounts specific to children. If you are attempting to reach the local military community, you can offer discounts to active-duty personnel, veterans, and their families. If you are having an evening program, you can choose groups that represent your target audience, such as young-professional networking groups, and offer discounts to them. You can offer as many or as few discounts as you wish, but those discounts can be a useful tool to help you reach your goals.

Some museums have removed their admission charges in an effort to eliminate barriers for their visitors. This is particularly useful for regional museums that are focused on serving their nearby communities. Those institutions don't want anyone to avoid visiting due simply to the cost. The goal is to send a welcoming message that everyone is invited to the museum. Eliminating admission charges also allows new visitors who aren't sure if they like museums to attend with little risk. They can plan to come for twenty minutes if they are not sure if they will enjoy the experience. The commitment is low, but hopefully the experience is excellent. Free admission is usually funded by endowments from generous donors who believe that museums should be accessible for all. If your admission is free, make sure that is a key part of your marketing. If people believe your museum's admission is expensive, they may choose not to visit.

As the Chrysler Museum of Art was considering moving to a full free-admission model, it had free admission on Wednesdays. One Wednesday, an anonymous note was placed in the donation box. The note helped solidify the museum's goal of full free admission and showcased how free admission could help them achieve their vision. The small but impactful note said this:

> Thank you for your free Wednesdays. My grandson and I each made a $1.00 donation and I purchased a toy spectrograph for $2.05. After my rent, utilities, and medications and before any other living or transportation expense, this small amount is more than 1% of my monthly income. My circumstances make inexpensive things like cable or internet as well as expensive things such as dental care and eyeglasses out of my reach. This is not a complaint. I hope this explains why this provision is so important. A visit here is so enriching to my heart and mind.

## VISITOR COMFORT

Operating in a visitor-centric way means prioritizing the comfort of your visitors as you make museum decisions. If you do things right, people don't always notice, but if you get things wrong, your visitors will be frustrated. People don't often comment that the signage was clear, that there was a bench right where they needed it, or that they were able to travel through the museum with ease. They simply enjoy the experience. However, they certainly notice when those things aren't true, and their experiences are diminished.

In addition to the items below, you should always be thinking of visitors when you make scheduling decisions. If you have to complete tasks that will impact the public areas, you must stop to consider the impact on your visitors. Consider activities that will close galleries or be noisy. Is there a way to do this work while the museum is closed? Are there other ways to reduce the impact? It's not always possible to eliminate the effect on visitors, but you want to minimize it as much as possible.

### Seating

For many people, a museum visit can be physically draining due to the amount of time spent standing and walking. If your visitors get too tired, they may lean on your displays, which is clearly dangerous, or they may cut their visits short and miss out on the experience of your museum. This means seating needs to be a priority, even if it impacts the space available for display objects.

You will need a variety of furniture options because one seating solution will not serve all your visitors' needs. People have different abilities, heights, preferences, and visiting patterns. For many museums, a variety of benches, chairs, and portable stools work well together. Furniture selections should be based primarily on visitor comfort, not simply appearance.

Backless benches can accommodate several people and are versatile in areas where people may want to face multiple directions. This flexibility means these benches are one of the most common types of seating found in museums. If you can invest in only one style of furniture, this is probably your best option. Whenever possible, you should choose padded benches to add comfort for your visitors so your visitors can rest for longer periods of time. For practical reasons, you also want a sturdy fabric that is easy to clean, such as leather or faux leather.

In addition to backless benches, you should look for options with back support. Larger furniture items with backs, such as sofas or backed benches, work in only some areas in your museum since these benches can face only one direction and sofas can take up a lot of space. These items can be placed back-to-back in larger galleries to increase the viewing possibilities. Benches or sofas can also be placed against walls in areas where there are not objects on display on the walls. Round sofas offer a fun option in large lobbies or other large, open areas. A small number of these furniture pieces can go a long way.

Individual chairs are also nice options that offer back support. If a chair is available with and without arms, it's best to get a mix of options. Some visitors may find it much easier to stand up with the use of the arms, and larger visitors may feel more comfortable without the constraint of arms. Many visitors will choose either of these options without much thought, whichever is closest or most convenient. However, those who have specific needs or preferences will be able to find seats that work for them.

Portable stools can round out your seating options and they offer flexibility that other options can't. Stools allow seating anywhere in your museum for participating in a program, sketching, doing homework, watching a video, or simply enjoying an exhibition that doesn't include a seat in that specific location. This seating option may allow people with less stamina to stay with their groups. It is worth investing in high-quality stools that are sturdy and have handles visitors can use for assistance standing up.

As you choose furniture, you should look carefully at the specifications. Note the seat height for each piece. For some visitors, the lower they must go to get to a bench or chair, the harder it is to stand back up. The Americans with Disabilities Act recommends bench heights of seventeen to nineteen inches.[1] If the furniture you are interested in comes in a few height options, consider a height that is on the higher end. You should always look for sturdy, low-maintenance options with the highest weight limit possible in order to accommodate the

**Figure 5.1.** *Source: Chrysler Museum of Art*

highest number of individuals. If possible, get samples of your proposed seating options and have your staff, volunteers, and even visitors try them out. Be sure to test them with people of different ages, body types, and abilities, and be open to feedback.

You've now selected the perfect furniture, but it won't matter if these perfect seats aren't in the right locations. There are a few key locations in your museum for you to consider.

The first place to add seating is in your galleries, where people naturally want to linger and enjoy the content. Consider placement near videos, works or installations that visitors want to ponder for a longer time, natural places for people to sketch, and interactive activities. If you are unsure where these locations are, the staff members who work in your public spaces will know.

You also should add seating in places where visitors might naturally want to wait for other members of their parties. This includes inside entrances, outside exhibitions, in central areas between exhibitions, and near the museum store. If you do not provide seating in these locations, you will find people get frustrated while they wait or rush their companions.

Look for at least one location that can function as a hub of activity. This area may include seating options, reading material, and videos or other activities. This is an area where people can gather, and it's a great place for people watching. Food and drink should be permitted if possible because that allows people to linger longer. You can have more than one of these areas, but you need at least one.

Throughout your museum, you should place benches and other seating options with enough frequency to prevent visitors from leaning on pedestals or display cases. In most museums, seating should appear roughly in every other gallery. In practicality, you may have seating for several galleries in a row, then a section without, but having a rough idea helps you plan.

Your portable stools can help you adapt and add seating quickly. Racks that hold these stools are generally on wheels and can be moved to convenient locations as needed. If something new is added to the galleries, you have the option of placing a couple stools in the area or mounting a few stools on a wall near the new display.

## Visitor Guide

The majority of museums allow their visitors to explore unescorted, so your visitor guide is an important tool people can carry with them. These guides are traditionally printed, but museums have also begun offering their guides in a digital format, usually with a code that can be scanned at the welcome desk. You can serve the widest range of visitors by offering both options. You save paper when visitors are happy to use their phones and still offer a printed guide for others. The printed option may be preferred by visitors who are less tech savvy, people who find paper easier to read than screens, or visitors whose phone batteries are dying. No matter the format, your visitor guide should include a clear map, museum policies, information about amenities, and answers to frequently asked questions.

A clear map is a key element of the guide. Your map should be large enough to read and include enough detail to allow for easy wayfinding but not be cluttered with excess information. Be sure to label all amenities, including restrooms (clearly marking gender-neutral or family restrooms), elevators, stairs, ramps, entrances, the museum store, and food-service options. Use icons in addition to labels. You want the map to be useful for those who speak different languages or who use different terms based on regional differences. This may seem like a tedious process, but it's essential. I once visited a museum that didn't label the restrooms on their map. It was frustrating for me and many other visitors, although I had an enjoyable experience with strangers as we hunted for the rooms together.

You also want to label specific content areas or exhibitions. You should consider coloring these areas of the map to make it easy for visitors to understand. Try to use colors with enough contrast to be useful for visitors who are color-blind. When describing different exhibitions or areas of interest, use thumbnail images for those who may not recognize vocabulary or an exhibition title. A small image may pique people's interest and help them plan their visit.

The same language should be used in wall-mounted maps and signs as in your printed visitor guide. While internally you may refer to one space with many names, be sure to choose one name for public use. One space may go by the names Impressionist Gallery, Gallery 212, and the Sally Jones Gallery. The museum store may also be called the gift shop or museum shop. The restaurant may be listed as the restaurant or café or by its specific name. In all these cases, you need to choose which name you will use for visitor information and stick with it. When in doubt, pick the simplest option.

There are a few common questions that should be addressed in your guide. If your museum is named after a person or has an otherwise unique name, the explanation of why it has that name should be included. Sometimes we assume everyone knows the story, but many visitors are left wondering. People will want to know also about the history of your building and museum. Did your building serve another purpose before it was a museum? Did your museum have a different name or location? Your visitors are curious about these questions. You also need to note where visitors can go for information. Is there a central information desk or a team of people they should reach out to with questions? If they should go to a desk, mark the desk on your map with a question mark. If they should go to a team, describe the team members' uniforms and include a photograph if possible. Ask your frontline staff about other common questions as they are your experts in this area.

You will need to include hours and important information about your amenities, including dining options and the museum store. For dining, a brief description is useful. It's good for visitors to know if they are encountering a cafeteria or a white-tablecloth restaurant. You should include information about key programs such as daily tours, demonstrations, family days, or exciting evening programs.

You should list also any key policies. As will be discussed later in this book, people who are corrected for breaking rules are more likely to walk away with negative memories of their visits. For example, if you don't allow photography in certain areas, you should share that with visitors. No one likes to feel foolish or embarrassed because they didn't know. If food or drink are not permitted in the theater, share that information up front.

If you have the resources, you should offer the visitor guide in additional languages (prioritize languages based on your community and visitors), in large print, and in braille. For these versions, you may want to simplify the information so it stays accurate for a longer period of time. You can also create a children's version that helps young visitors navigate the museum and explains policies in a kid-friendly way.

**Signage**

We have all had the experience of feeling lost. It's stressful and can put a true damper on an experience. In addition to the clear map in the visitor guide, you will need wayfinding signage to help visitors navigate during their visits. These signs need to be carefully created, and this process is a great opportunity for collaboration between your visitor-services team and your communications department. You want your signs to be attractive and easy to read, but most importantly, they need to be in the right locations.

As you consider the appearance of your signs, you will want to adhere to your museum's brand standards. You also want to ensure readability by making sure that the contrast between the lettering and background is strong, the font is easy to read, and the text is large enough to be read by your visitors.

The visit begins as soon as someone arrives on your campus, and your signs will welcome your visitors outside of your museum. Consider each direction that visitors will arrive from, paying close attention to the directions that most GPS systems use. If those systems guide visitors to the side of the building, make sure there are clear signs in that area directing visitors to the parking lot. From the parking lot, you'll need directions to the main entrance. For some museums, finding the entrance can be more confusing than for others. If there are multiple entrances, make sure to clearly label the one you want visitors to use. The correct entrance may not be as obvious as you think it is.

Inside the museum, your signs should include directions to popular amenities and exhibitions. As mentioned above, you need to be consistent in the language you use. The names for various areas of your museum should match the map in your visitor guide. Be sure to clearly label restrooms so visitors can find those quickly. While you don't want to overwhelm visitors with too many signs, some museums go too minimal at a detriment to their visitors. A clean aesthetic is not worth frustrated visitors.

If possible, create mockups of your signs and post them in the final signs' locations. Are they easy to read from the position or distance where visitors will likely be viewing them? Have you taken all routes into consideration? Could some signs be combined in order to save space? Test the readability with a variety of people to see what needs to be changed.

As you move forward, you should never consider your signage project truly complete. You should be open to feedback, observe your visitors, and make changes as necessary.

## PERSONAL PREFERENCES

As mentioned in previous chapters, people who run museums do not generally represent typical museum visitors. Unfortunately, we often think we do. We design experiences based on our preferences, but we need to actively consider the varying preferences of our visitors and design experiences that are flexible and can fulfill all their needs.

This concept applies to most activities. No matter the attraction, each person will have his or her own style that allows for the most individual enjoyment. For example, if you asked amusement-park enthusiasts about planning their park visits, you would hear many different approaches, and each person would likely believe his or her way was best. Some visitors would arrive before the park opens, have the entire day meticulously planned, pack a picnic lunch to save money, and be sure to visit every area of the park. Others would come for just a few hours to ride every roller coaster and eat a leisurely meal in the park whenever they get hungry. Both sets of people would walk away having enjoyed the day, but they may not have enjoyed a day planned by the other group.

This same principle applies to museums. As mentioned before, if museums want to truly prioritize diversity, they can't just tolerate the differences among their visitors; they need to embrace those differences. Your visitors will have varying levels of expertise, move at different paces, engage in distinct ways, have diverse interests, and travel through the museum in different ways.

Some visitors enjoy thoroughly discussing the exhibition topics with people and others may want a solitary, introspective experience. Some visitors may want someone to guide or plan their visit and others want to explore on their own. There are visitors who want to see every item in a museum for a brief moment each and others want to spend their entire visit in their favorite area. Neither option is wrong, and you want your museum to be able to accommodate each preference. Allowing visitors to spend their time with the items that mean the most to them leads to higher visitor satisfaction.

In a real example, a historic home offered only one type of visit: guided tours on the hour. If a visitor arrived fifteen minutes into the hour, he or she was directed to come back later, even if no one was on a current tour and the tour guide was available. The tour was one set pattern, with time for brief questions but no time to dive deeply into any specific topic.

The institution's leaders decided to assess the tour as part of a plan to improve the visitor experience. They were surprised to discover that approximately half of the visitors who were turned away due to arriving at the wrong time did not come back and found something else to do with their day. They also discovered that some people wanted extra time in specific rooms or more information on specific topics, and there was no way to accommodate that. No matter how much those visitors enjoyed the rest of the tour, they were disappointed about this, and it impacted their overall view of their experience.

The leaders also wanted to know which topics were most popular with visitors so they could design the one perfect tour. They discovered that the results were incredibly varied. Different respondents prioritized learning about the life of the family, the enslaved servants who worked in the home, the military connections, the architecture of the home, and more. There was no one perfect tour.

They designed a new framework that allowed visitors to either receive a guided tour or explore the home on their own. Tours are now available on a rolling basis, and while tour guides have a general outline with an assortment of information, they are ready to pivot and follow the interests of the visitors. If a visitor wants to learn about the lives of the enslaved servants, the guide is ready with additional stories and letters and may take the visitors to a different part of the home. If people are interested in architecture, they may be guided to an area of exposed brick that shows the building additions over time. The addition of a self-guided option required some physical changes to the home including adding vitrines over a few small objects, adding stanchions, and producing some additional printed didactics. Having these options available has led to deeper experiences for visitors, higher attendance, and higher visitor-satisfaction ratings.

## ACCESSIBILITY

As you plan for your visitors' needs, you must include the 26 percent of the population who has some type of disability.[2] Of course, museums meet the minimum requirements set by the Americans with Disabilities Act, but the goal is to go beyond that to provide the best possible experience for everyone.

It's important to speak directly with individuals with disabilities in order to learn how you can make your museum more accessible and enjoyable for each of them. There often are local organizations that you could partner with and learn from. If you build these relationships, you can create an ongoing open dialogue to help you improve.

Some individuals need physical assistance moving through your museum and may utilize wheelchairs, walkers, scooters, or canes. These individuals may need ramps or elevators to enter your building rather than staircases. Accessible options should be as close to the main entrance as possible as the goal is for the welcome to be the same for all visitors. If these visitors come through a separate entrance, look for ways to make that area feel the same as the main entrance. Be sure handrails are plentiful and sturdy. Many people need a little help stabilizing themselves and you don't want people to grab pedestals instead.

A museum visit is a physical activity, so some people may prefer to use wheelchairs even if they don't on a day-to-day basis. It is best to offer loaners to allow visitors to maximize their experiences. Standard push wheelchairs are relatively easy to use with little experience, but scooters are more challenging. This makes scooters difficult to loan as they could be dangerous in museum galleries. It makes more sense to offer them at large outdoor museums.

Videos are important in museums and often add context to your content. Be sure your videos include captions for visitors who are deaf or hard of hearing as well as audio for visitors who are blind or have low vision. People who need vision accessibility can benefit also from audio tours, large-print labels (perhaps in a simple binder available at the welcome desk or in the galleries), or large-print visitor guides.

Some museums can be overwhelming for visitors with sensory disabilities. In addition to the sensory-friendly hours mentioned earlier, you can also offer spaces to take a break, noise-canceling headphones to eliminate background noise, and fidget toys to allow these visitors to focus and enjoy their visits.

An important component to welcoming people with disabilities is to train your frontline staff to welcome and serve each individual. This training will be discussed in chapter 10.

## VISITOR-FOCUSED AMENITIES

The experience of visiting a museum is more than just seeing the wonderful objects on the walls; it's a well-rounded experience that includes time with loved ones, self-discovery, and, as pointed out in chapter 2, fun.

For those who may not feel comfortable in museums, amenities such as the museum store or the restaurant may help put them at ease. Shopping and dining are familiar experiences that can help visitors adapt to the unfamiliar experience of a museum.

Other amenities are there to make the experience as comfortable as possible for everyone. These amenities can help people feel comfortable, and once visitors' basic needs are taken care of, people are open to great experiences.

### Dining Options

Food is something that connects us all. Everyone needs to eat, and many people enjoy trying new food, talking about food, and even taking photographs of their food. If strangers find themselves trying to make conversation, food is a great topic on which they can often find common ground. This is why dining experiences can be important.

The food-service opportunities at some museums are utilitarian. If you must eat while you are there, there is something available for purchase. At other institutions, the restaurant is a true culinary destination with its own identity. Whether your institution offers one or both options or something in between, food service can be an important component of a visit to your museum.

Consider how your museum's food service matches your visitors and their preferences. If your primary audience is families with young children, a formal, fine-dining experience may not be the best fit. It may be better to offer fast, simple options. On the other end of the spectrum, if your visitors tend to enjoy a more formal environment, they may prefer a restaurant with more elaborate service. In addition to formality and price preferences, you also may want to consider the length of the average visit and how dining matches that time. If visits are short, there should be dining options that are also quick. If visitors come for the entire day, they may enjoy a leisurely meal to break up the day.

If your museum is busy enough, it's ideal to offer multiple dining options that meet the preferences of more visitors. If you are trying to make one option work for many people, you may want to be sure there is as much variety as possible. This might mean that it's seated service, but the restaurant also has a children's menu and there are some simple to-go options.

## Museum Store

Similar to dining experiences, shopping excursions are something relatable to most people and a component of the visitor experience that many people look forward to.

Does the store experience match their overall visit? There should be a clear connection between the rest of the visit and the culminating experience in the store. The store is the only portion of the museum that visitors can take with them, so you want to be sure the visit ends on a positive note and ideally with the perfect souvenir to take home.

Within the store, what is the experience like? Museum stores vary from a bookshelf near the admission desk to a multilevel store that covers thousands of square feet. What do visitors see first? A great museum store will have products at a variety of price points. If visitors see a wall of very expensive items when they first walk in, they may decide the store isn't for them and walk right out. The same may happen if parents see a large display of breakable items. Be sure the first thing people see as they approach the store doesn't give the wrong impression. Since a good store has a variety of items, can visitors clearly identify and locate the sections and products that may appeal to them?

## Areas for Parents and Children

Families may have different needs as they visit your museum, and you want to be sure you have areas that meet their needs. While parents are certainly welcome to feed their babies anywhere in your museum, you may want to dedicate an area to allow privacy for those who prefer it, particularly for nursing mothers. You should also be sure there are diaper-changing stations in every restroom, including men's restrooms. If your sinks are high, consider fold-down steps that allow children to step up and wash their hands independently.

You may also have areas that are designed for children's activities. These could range from a simple craft area to an elaborate, interactive play area. Be sure there is seating in these areas that is suitable for both adults and children and is easy to clean. Parents may have strollers or large diaper bags with them, so make sure these areas can easily accommodate those items. These areas should be designed for all children, including those with disabilities. Be sure this area is easy to navigate for everyone and easy for families to find.

## Coat Checks and Lockers

It's best for you to have free or inexpensive areas for visitors to store belongings as they explore the museum. This adds to their basic comfort, which can extend and improve their visits and helps you protect your collection. If people are carrying bulky coats, large bags, or backpacks through your galleries, they are more likely to bump works or displays. You may offer these services as options for visitors who don't want to carry these items, or you may require that people leave them due to your visitor policies. Either way, these areas should be easy to find and use.

A complimentary coat check is an easy way to accommodate items of all sizes, and many people feel comfortable leaving their items with staff members. Depending on the size of your museum, the coat check may be a separate area, or it may be located near the main entrance or admission desk so it doesn't require an additional staff person. Lockers offer an option for those who don't want others to handle their items. These should also be free or inexpensive. Lockers may also be useful if you don't have an easy area to use for coat check.

Coat checks and lockers are an area where you need to be consistent with your policies. If some visitors are told that they can't take items such as umbrellas, water bottles, or shopping bags with them into the galleries, they are likely to be upset if they see other visitors carrying these items. It's also upsetting if they get past the entrance and a staff member informs them of this rule further into the visit.

## Access to Water

You want your visitors to easily be able to find something to drink. Preventing dehydration can help visitors extend their visits. If you allow visitors to carry water bottles through the museum, you should have places to easily purchase disposable water bottles and have a station for visitors to fill their reusable bottles. This is also an opportunity for the museum store to sell branded reusable bottles to visitors. If you do not allow water bottles in your galleries, you still need to find a way to offer water to your visitors. Traditionally, drinking fountains have filled this need. If you think your visitors may not be comfortable with this shared amenity, you may want to find an option that includes disposable cups. However you choose to offer water, be sure it is easy to find, particularly on hot days.

## Pulling It All Together

As you work toward the goal of offering a cohesive, comfortable, and visitor-centric experience, you need to frequently put yourself in the shoes of your visitors. Physically touring your facility, when the museum is both open and closed, allows you to see problems and make improvements.

Walk through your museum as a visitor, starting outside the museum. Is it easy to find the main entrance from the parking lot? Does the entrance feel welcoming? As you maneuver through the museum, pay attention to the locations of signs. Are signs in the right locations to help you? Are seating options in the right locations? Is anything confusing? This is similar to the exercise you did as you completed your journey map, but you are looking for finer details this time.

In addition to walking through the building, tour the building in a wheelchair. If you offer loaner chairs, you can borrow one of those. This will give you a glimpse into the challenges of visiting your museum in a wheelchair. Are some turns tight? Is the museum store crowded with fixtures? Are some ramps steeper than others? Is any of the flooring difficult to roll on? You also need to pay attention to the height of cases, objects, and labels. Can a visitor in a wheelchair see and experience everything in your galleries?

This exercise can prevent mistakes that impact your visitors, such as historic books being displayed at an angle that can't be seen from a wheelchair or signage arrows that get you only partway to your destination.

I once visited a museum where, due to inclement weather, visitors were directed to an alternative entrance so they could quickly reach the coat-check area. This altered the general traffic flow through the museum, and the foyer where visitors would typically begin their visits was now where they concluded. This area included an information desk and audio-tour options. I wasn't aware of these offerings, and from what I overheard, neither were many fellow visitors. The staff who made this change were likely focused on the need to make coat check a smooth and simple process, but they did not consider the whole picture. A walk-through may have prevented this.

If you have museum colleagues in your city who you have a good relationship with, you can help each other and lend fresh eyes to one another's museums. They may see something that you've missed. It can often be easier to see these difficulties in others' museums than in your own, and you will be able to learn from one another's strengths.

You also need to take the time to observe your visitors and see how they travel through the museum. You want to understand the natural traffic flow, which may not be the pattern you have designed. Some visitors start with their favorites, some start with what's new, some move chronologically, and some deliberately go against the flow of others. Be prepared for visitors to move in any direction. From your observations, where are there bottlenecks or points of confusion? Are there barriers to participation for some individuals? At decision points where visitors can choose from multiple directions, which way do they choose? Where do visitors want to linger to look at an object or read a label? Is there room for multiple people to look at the same time? Try to spread out your most popular works to avoid crowds. As you look ahead, you may have to do this exercise as you plan for upcoming events or exhibitions. As an exhibition is installed, you should complete the exercise again to ask the same questions.

To get a true picture of your visitors, you also need to observe individuals and groups of all sizes, including school tours, adult tour groups, and families. You also should observe on different days, in different seasons, and when different exhibitions are on display. A very popular exhibition may change typical visitor behavior, and school tours may gather in different spaces than other groups do.

To build a complete picture, you need to combine your observations from this exercise with the data you gathered in chapters 3 and 4. While all sources are valuable, the frontline staff are likely your best resource when it comes to information about your visitors. In the example above about changing the entrance to be closer to coat check, the staff likely knew that there was a problem with the new traffic flow. They probably heard complaints right away but may not have had a clear line of communication to the museum's decision-makers.

Now that your museum is set up to welcome your visitors, it's time to consider what service means to you.

## NOTES

1. "903 Benches," *ADA Compliance Directory*, ADA Compliance, https://www.ada-compliance.com/ada-compliance/903-benches

2. "Disability Impacts All of Us," Centers for Disease Control and Prevention, https://www.cdc.gov/ncbddd/disabilityandhealth/documents/disabilities_impacts_all_of_us.pdf

# 6

## Articulating What Service Means to You

You have likely put some thought into the type of service you want to extend to your visitors. Some of the ideas mentioned in this book may sound like they are a great fit for you, and others may not fit your institution. It's important that you find your own voice and clearly communicate your service principles to your frontline team and throughout your institution.

### WHAT ARE SERVICE PRINCIPLES?

Service principles are the key factors you feel define your specific style of service. These might read as a list or an acronym of three to eight words or phrases that are important to you and represent the type of visitor experience you want to offer. This puts the large concept of service into something more focused and easier to understand. Depending on the final product, this list may also be referred to as a service model.

You may have a bulleted list of items that are meaningful to you and guide your operations. A simple example may look something like this:

- Greet every visitor
- Be sure everyone feels welcome
- Share everyone's history
- Love learning

If these were your principles, you would probably spend time in training talking about how you wanted visitors to be greeted, both at the main entrance and as they enter various spaces throughout the museum, such as exhibitions or the museum store. For the next item, you would likely discuss how to create a welcoming environment for a diverse audience. This may also guide those who are designing your exhibitions so they prioritize a welcoming environment that serves multiple audiences. When you state that you share everyone's history, you may be referring to showcasing many stories. If your site includes a historic home, you are not simply telling the story of the wealthy man who lived there, but you are also sharing the stories of the women in the family and the enslaved servants who worked in the home. The last item makes it clear that you are an educational institution that values lifelong learning. You also encourage your staff to continue learning about your collection.

You may also choose to use an acronym, which can organize your thoughts in a way that is easy for your team to remember. You may showcase the ART of customer service. This could be presented in the following way:

Adapt service to each individual
Relationships are key
Treat everyone with respect

If this were your model, you would use the *A* to talk about recognizing differences among your visitors and adapting your service. As you discuss the *R*, you would talk about how you strive to build relationships with regular visitors and members. These relationships are focused on long-term goals and growing these connections over time. The *T* is straightforward, and you may want to take time to define what respect means to you.

A list may not be the right fit for you. You may decide that a simple statement defines what you are trying to accomplish and guides your decision-making. The statement could be something like, "We believe every citizen of Smalltown should feel pride and ownership of this museum." This statement shows that the goal is to connect and engage with the local community.

Once the work is complete, your list of principles or service model should be used as the basic structure of your frontline-staff training, should be a guide for decision-making throughout the institution, and should be displayed where it can be seen by a variety of staff members. Your list of principles represents your institution's service and experience goals, and it impacts all aspects of museum operations.

## WHY NOT ONE UNIVERSAL MODEL?

While many museums could thrive on a basic, universal service model, this chapter is focused on finding the unique voice of your museum. There are some ideas that would likely be included in many institutions' service models, but you will decide if those describe your museum and build from there. These universal ideas could include a warm welcome, prioritizing diversity and accessibility, embracing learning, and removing barriers that prevent visitation. Those are all positive thoughts, but you also want to add items that are specific to your museum.

Your community and your unique visitors will likely have an impact on what your distinctive service and desired experience will look like. This is one of the reasons it is so important to learn about your visitors, as discussed in chapter 3. Do you serve more tourists or your local community? Are you on a university campus? Are your visitors experienced museumgoers or novices? Do most of your visitors attend with families or on their own? How experienced are your visitors with your content? Everything you can learn about your visitors will help you tailor a great visitor experience.

As you go through the process of defining your service principles, remember that it's important your principles be not only a reflection of who your museum currently is but also an aspirational statement of who you want it to be.

# DETERMINING YOUR OWN SERVICE PRINCIPLES

There are a few ways you can approach the creation of your service principles. You may want leaders from the visitor experience team to prepare a draft for others to review, or you may want to gather a cross-departmental group to get input from several sources. Whatever approach you choose depends on your workplace culture and everyone's availability. Will you have more buy-in if more people are able to participate? If so, include as many people as possible up front. This is especially important if your organization is making a large philosophical shift. If your departments function somewhat independently, it may make more sense to create a draft to share.

No matter which group completes this process, the exercise will be largely the same. The exercise will usually be led by your director of visitor services or someone in a similar position. If you are looking beyond your department, you should consider including senior leadership and anyone who is closely connected to the visitor experience, such as the museum store manager, director of education, food and beverage manager, security manager, and leaders from the frontline staff. Each of these individuals will have a different perspective that is valuable. If you include people only within your department, be sure to choose the best representatives from your frontline team.

The goal of this part of the exercise is to gather everyone's thoughts about the types of service and experience you want for your visitors. You can either gather as a group to accomplish this or interview all stakeholders separately with the questions below and combine the answers later. If you have a large group you want to include, or you believe there will be differing opinions, you can greatly benefit from interviewing people separately or breaking into small groups. Some individuals are less likely to speak up in a group, particularly if they disagree. If you are embarking on this task because you are looking for a drastic change or you feel there is something to fix, it is best to do individual interviews.

## Gathering Your Thoughts

Begin with sticky notes of a single color and write each word or phrase that comes up from the questions below on a separate note. Don't worry about wordsmithing or using complete sentences at this stage. Just write things in the natural language that everyone uses. It's OK if things come up more than once; either make separate notes or make tick marks on the note to indicate popularity. This likely shows something that is important to your institution.

## Questions and Discussion Topics

Start with your mission statement, vision statement, core values, strategic plan, and any other institutional documents that are fundamental to your organization. Are there ideas in them that relate to service or the visitor experience? Some examples are phrases like "inform and inspire," "enrich and transform lives," "we love science," or "we value diversity."

How do you want visitors to feel in your museum? Do you want them to feel welcome? Do you want them to feel like they belong? Do you want them to feel comfortable?

As you describe your ideal service team, what comes to mind? Friendly people? People who are passionate about your mission? People who value learning? People who can form connections with new people?

Are there things about your current visitor experience that you would like to change? Do some people not feel welcome? Do visitors report a negative experience with staff? Is rule enforcement always a negative experience?

Give some serious thought to diversity, accessibility, equity, and inclusion. These are important considerations for all museums, but what do they mean to you? Are there disparities between your community and your visitors? How can your service and on-site experience help change that? Do visitors see themselves reflected in your frontline team? in your senior staff? in your board? Is your museum welcoming to visitors with disabilities? What about intellectual accessibility—is your content truly aimed at your visitors or does it exclude some individuals? It is essential that these concepts are present in some way in your service model.

Your frontline staff will need to make decisions without you as you can't possibly tell them what to do in each scenario. As they make these decisions, what do you want them to keep in mind? How should they handle unusual requests? Is consistency important to you or is flexibility? Do staff have some freedom to make their own decisions?

Is your museum focused on one prescribed experience? Visitors are unique and will often want to experience your museum differently. How will you accommodate this? Do you offer programs to allow for these differences?

Are there real or perceived barriers that prevent people from visiting? For some, these may be straightforward barriers such as the price of admission, lack of public transportation, or difficult parking. There also could be barriers that are more difficult to overcome. Do people see your museum differently from how you do? Do they view your museum as elitist or exclusionary? Have they had previous negative experiences? How can you break through these barriers to reach more of your community?

At their core, museums are educational institutions. How do you demonstrate your commitment to learning? Is it by offering engaging educational programming? By speaking to visitors with varying levels of expertise? By prioritizing education for children?

As you wrap up, you also should ask if anyone has any other words or phrases they feel should be included that haven't already been discussed. You want everyone to feel like they were able to voice their opinions.

## Grouping Similar Responses

Once you have all your thoughts written down, your next step is to take the sticky notes and group them with similar items. Figure 6.1 shows a simple example of this process. You see several sticky notes with similar ideas grouped together. For example, you see "warm," "welcoming," "friendly," "approachable," and "hospitality" together as a united concept.

Once you've grouped your initial thoughts, grab a set of sticky notes in a different color and try to create headings that convey the message from each group of notes. These headings may or may not be the same as what is written on one of the notes. In figure 6.1, the first group may be titled "warm welcome" or "hospitality."

Set to the side anything that doesn't fit with the other responses or with your desired direction. Do not discard these just yet; they are valuable and will be discussed later.

## Finalizing Your Principles

Now it's time to put those ideas into a form that is easy to communicate. Once complete, this can be a basis for training, a simple way to communicate to new employees and other

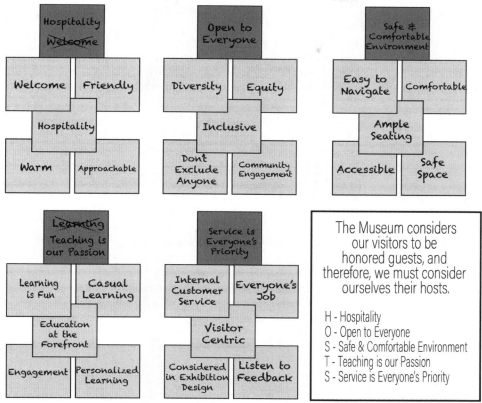

**Figure 6.1.** *Courtesy of Author*

stakeholders, and a document to reference when making institutional decisions. As previously mentioned, your goal is to end up with three to eight words or phrases that represent the type of service you want to offer your visitors. If you have more than eight groups of sticky notes, take a second look to see if you can group anything together further. If your list of principles is too long, it will be difficult to remember and won't have the impact that you are looking for.

Once you've decided on your short list, you'll need to convert it into a simple form that is easy to communicate. First you need to decide what format you will use. As mentioned above, common formats are a list, an acronym, an alliterated list, or a strong statement. You could call your list "the top five service values," "the SCIENCE of service," or "the six *P*s of museum service."

Acronyms can be useful if you incorporate the initials of your institution or a word that relates to your mission or to service. Once you decide to use an acronym, you may have to play a little with the headings you chose. If you want words that begin with a certain letter, you may have to swap the word "welcome" for "hospitality" or vice versa. If you need help wordsmithing or brainstorming synonyms, look to the talented writers you likely have on your museum staff and ask for their assistance.

In figure 6.1, three of the headings begin with the letters *O* or *S*. We see that with a few adjustments, we can make the acronym HOSTS, which may define how you want your staff to treat visitors. Changing "welcome" to "hospitality" and "learning" to "teaching" makes the phrase easy to share with everyone.

If there are particular phrases you want to include, such as "learning is fun" or "we love science," don't sacrifice what you really want to say for the sake of a catchy slogan. It's great if the slogan does fit, but if it doesn't, you still can get your point across with a straightforward list.

The next step is to transform your words into something that is graphically interesting. If your museum has a graphic designer on staff, that person is the perfect one to help you with this. Your designer understands your mission and can incorporate that into the graphic. If you use an outside designer, you will likely have to give a few more specifics about your institution. Either way, the goal is for someone to quickly understand who you are when it comes to service.

There are times you will want to expand and include more information than can be displayed in one graphic. It's handy to have a one-page document that is easy to read and explains the graphic in more detail. It may look similar to the Chrysler Museum of Art's example at the end of this chapter.

Once you have both your graphic and your explanation complete, share them with your museum's leadership and the others who participated in the process so you can get feedback. If you have any reason to believe that people will disagree with your final output, share the documents with your executive director first to be sure they agree with your assessment and you have support. If the principles represent a major change, it may be best if the executive director communicates the new direction to staff.

### Ideas That Are Not Included

Naturally, you will not be able to include every idea from each participant. Take a look at the concepts not included and be sure you understand why each was excluded. Common reasons for exclusion include an item being too repetitive, too detailed to be included at this broad level, or counter to what you are hoping to achieve. Look at all the notes that are not represented in your final graphic and determine which category they each fall into.

In some cases, an individual's precise words may not have been included, but the spirit of the opinion is present. Someone may feel strongly about including the word "diversity," but the group decided on language that mentions equity and a welcoming environment for everyone.

Some phrases can be too specific, but their thoughts can be included in other ways. For example, let's say someone was very focused on offering ample seating in public spaces. You may not include seating specifically in your final model, but you may list visitor comfort or accessibility. If someone was very passionate about this topic, consider calling it out in your longer explanation or in your training.

In other instances, someone's suggestion may oppose your goals. For example, if you have someone who thinks it's important for all visitors to follow one exact visit plan but your new philosophy highlights individuality, you know you may have a challenge ahead.

You also may find disagreement around intellectual accessibility. Some may feel that keeping items at a moderate reading level equates to talking down to visitors. They may prefer a more scholarly approach while others want to accommodate the largest number of visitors.

On paper, most museum professionals want to welcome new audiences. However, not everyone may agree with prioritizing new people as highly as existing visitors. Some museum workers also may not like that novice visitors will often be unfamiliar with the museum's content or the museum's rules. Welcoming more first-time visitors may lead to a learning curve with the scholarly content and more frequent rule breaking and potential incidents in the galleries. When rules are broken, the enforcement method also may be up for debate. Some people may prefer harsher methods to make a strong statement, while others may want to show empathy and patience as new visitors learn about your museum.

When someone's opinion opposes your new service statements, you will have to clearly explain the decisions to try to get those individuals onboard. In these cases, you need to be sure you have the support of museum leadership to make your desired changes. It is also probably a good idea to talk to people with those opinions before the new model is released so they are not surprised. You want them to feel respected and connected to the process.

## SAMPLE SERVICE MODELS

### North Carolina Museum of Art

The North Carolina Museum of Art has shifted its priorities and streamlined its goals. Simply put, service over sales is its mission. This shift has really grown out of the team's desire to serve the community and an understanding of the bigger purpose of the museum campus.

The staff no longer determines success by the number of sales of tickets or merchandise. They look at how many new visitors they serve, how many free options on campus have been added, and how many community artisans they have added to their retail offerings.

### Chrysler Museum of Art

The Chrysler Museum of Art prides itself on offering SUPERB service. This acronym helps describe its style of service and goals for the visitor experience. SUPERB stands for the following:

Start with warmth
Understand your product
Positivity first
Engage with the individual
Respectful safeguarding
Beyond one department

*Start with warmth* invokes the spirit of hospitality that is at the core of the staff's goals for the visitor experience. In practice, this begins with their custom of opening the door for each visitor and is further reflected in the warm greeting, body language, and tone of voice of the team members who interact with visitors. This hospitality also prioritizes the comfort of visitors and making the museum accessible to visitors in every way.

*Understand your product* puts the focus on continuous learning for staff members. This includes learning about daily activities, programs, and frequently asked questions as well as learning more about the museum's collection, exhibitions, and art-making processes.

*Positivity first* refers to both how staff members convey policies and how they respond to requests. When answering questions about policies, they start with what visitors can do, not the negative list of what they can't. If someone has an unusual request, staff members ask themselves, "Can we say yes? Is there a way to accommodate this request or a portion of it?"

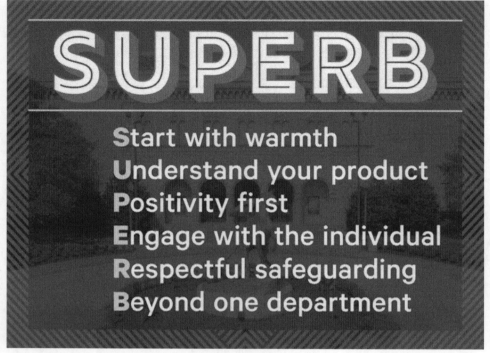

**SUPERB**

Start with warmth
Understand your product
Positivity first
Engage with the individual
Respectful safeguarding
Beyond one department

**Figure 6.2.** *Source: Chrysler Museum of Art*

Museum leaders want their staff to consider this when making decisions rather than simply defaulting to declining something that is not part of normal operations.

*Engage with the individual* signifies the goal of helping everyone have their own best visit to the museum. Not everyone will experience the museum in the same way, and staff aim to embrace all the ways visitors are unique and try to provide the best possible experience for each individual. Staff consider visitors' motivations for visiting the museum, art experience and expertise, and engagement preferences. They are also aware of welcoming groups that have traditionally been excluded from museums, confronting racial bias, welcoming the LGBTQIA+ community, working through language barriers, and serving people with disabilities.

*Respectful safeguarding* reflects something that the museum's leadership was looking to change when they created their gallery-host program. Rule enforcement needs to be consistent and firm but also can be polite and should not embarrass the visitor. By replacing traditional security officers in the galleries with people whose roles blend service, security, and engagement, staff change the method they use to enforce rules. Doing so takes what can be a negative experience and aims to change it into a positive one.

*Beyond one department* reinforces the message these service values not only are embraced by visitor services but also have a genuine commitment from the entire organization. Visitors' needs are considered in exhibition planning, programming, and all other aspects of museum operations.

# 7

# Determining the Structure
# of Your Frontline Team

A team is a group of individuals united by shared goals and objectives. Each museum staff member and volunteer belongs to multiple teams throughout the institution. The entire museum staff is one team working toward shared goals. Each department is a team, there are cross-departmental teams focused on specific topics, and everyone who interacts with your visitors is part of a frontline team tasked with providing excellent experiences. As visitors travel through your museum, they interact with many individuals, and they do not separate the staff into departments; in the minds of your visitors, all staff members are working together.

Look around your institution and be sure that the same level of service is provided by staff in all visitor-facing areas, including those areas operated by contractors. Consider how the service principles you developed could apply to your museum store, restaurant, theater, studio, and any other amenities you offer at your museum.

Experiencing vastly different levels of service is unsettling and confusing to visitors. If the first staff member visitors meet greets them warmly, talks about his or her favorite object, and offers to take photographs of visitors' families, visitors probably believe they are in a friendly place and they relax. If visitors are then sharply yelled at for breaking rules or snickered at for asking questions, their entire impression may change. If one bad apple spoils the bunch, one bad interaction can spoil a museum experience.

## DEFINING THE TEAM

Take a moment to consider who truly comprises your frontline team. Visitor services may come to mind first, but depending on the structure of your organization, there likely are many more people who have an impact on the visitor experience. All these people serve as ambassadors to your visitors and will be more successful working together.

### First Impressions

We all know that first impressions are important. What is the first impression for visitors as they arrive at your museum? Is it an enthusiastic, warm welcome? Do visitors walk into an

**Figure 7.1.   *Source: Chrysler Museum of Art***

empty hall on their own, unsure if they are in the right place? Are they harshly greeted with security searches? Think carefully about the first impression you want to give, who is at the door to greet your visitors, and what type of greeting is offered. These elements set the tone for the visitor experience.

For many museums, the ticketing process is an important component of the first impression and is one of the primary interactions with staff. While this is a relatively simple transaction, it is an important moment in the visitor experience. In addition to being a potential revenue opportunity, this welcome greatly influences the visit. The ticketing process may include an orientation to the museum, or this orientation may be handled separately by a different team of staff and volunteers. Either way, the orientation should be driven largely by the preferences of the visitor. Some visitors may want an elaborate welcome, a long conversation, and a suggested itinerary for their visit; others simply want a greeting and a map. Choose individuals for the orientation role who are able to adapt their services to different visitors, and train them to recognize these preferences in your visitors.

You want to be clear regarding your expectations with the ticketing process. The Philadelphia Museum of Art has developed a clear sequence of service that guides employees through the entire transaction. In addition to the ticket sale and orientation, this also includes providing information about membership and add-on opportunities for the visit. This ensures consistency while allowing employees to infuse their own personalities into the interaction.

The staff and volunteers at the entrance, the admission team, and those responsible for orientation are your first ambassadors and can have a profound impact on the experience of your visitors.

## Exit through the Museum Store

The museum store is a treasured component of the visitor experience. Many visitors look forward to visiting the store, usually at the end of the museum visit. The store visit is an opportunity to immediately reflect upon the museum experience and choose something to help them fondly remember the visit. The store should feel like an extension of the museum experience and not feel like a totally separate location. The service should match the institution's standards, and the staff should be knowledgeable about the museum as a whole.

Does your store reflect the complete visitor experience? Do visitors see their favorite objects reflected in the merchandise? The more connected your buyers and store staff are with the rest of the institution, the more your store will feel like a fundamental component of the museum. A well-designed museum store excites visitors as they enter, reminding them of everything they just experienced, and provides the perfect culmination to the visit.

The store provides a unique opportunity for visitors to take a piece of the museum home with them. The items visitors choose celebrate their visits and allow the museum to be part of their lives. These keepsakes provide an opportunity for visitors to discuss the items, and the museum, with friends and family in the future. Taking an item home also provides an opportunity for visitors to showcase their interests to the important people in their lives. For many, a love of art, history, animals, science, trains, or any other museum topic is something that they are proud of and something they want to share. They want these interests to be reflected in themselves and at home. Something as simple as a book on the coffee table, a unique piece of jewelry, or a tea towel hanging in the kitchen helps them showcase parts of their personalities. These items are more than trinkets; they allow the museum to become part of visitors' lives and identities.

## Don't Neglect the Middle

We've discussed first impressions as visitors enter the museum and the concluding experience in the museum store, and those are important bookends to the visit, but don't neglect everything in between.

Security officers that are present in public areas are part of your visitor experience team. Museums have multiple goals in placing officers in the galleries, including observing visitor behavior, enforcing rules, and providing an authoritative presence. All these goals can be accomplished while still providing excellent service. Security officers will be more successful if they feel like they are supported by the institution and related departments. Security practices are discussed further in the next chapter.

If food service is offered, it should feel like an extension of the institution. The atmosphere should match the feel of your museum. As mentioned previously, if you have a museum geared toward casual family experiences, a high-end fine-dining restaurant may seem out of place. You need to tailor the dining style to your visitors. No matter what style of restaurant you offer, you need to be sure the service matches your standards.

The staff who work in the restaurant should feel connected to the museum as a whole, even if they work for an outside contractor. Being offered tours of the collection and discounts on tickets and memberships can help the food-service team feel that connection. This team will need to be able to answer questions about the museum, so be sure to provide them with the answers to frequently asked questions as well as someone to turn to for more complicated issues. To encourage good service with a contractor, you can clearly communicate your standards and offer incentives based on visitor-satisfaction scores. These incentives could include reduced commission fees or extended lease renewals.

Visitors spend the majority of their time in your gallery spaces, so it's important to consider their experience there, including interactions with staff and volunteers. While many visitors enjoy discovering museum treasures on their own, they may also enjoy some guidance and additional information to help in their understanding of the topics and to make the objects come to life. Look for ways to add engagement to your galleries, such as ambassadors offering help, gallery attendants answering questions, demonstrations throughout the day, or opportunities for hands-on activities. These are opportunities to surprise and delight your visitors with unexpected information and experiences.

## BRINGING THE TEAMS TOGETHER

Your organizational chart may list the groups above separately, but all groups are working together to serve your visitors. The visitor experience will be more successful if the teams view themselves as being one larger team in addition to being smaller departmental teams. You can encourage this viewpoint in multiple ways.

### Working Together

If you want your frontline teams to feel connected to one another, look for opportunities for them to work together. Everyone needs to know about daily activities, so the morning meeting or a printed agenda should be shared. The topics discussed could include tour groups attending that day, program details, expected visitation, recent concerns, and other relevant information. The meeting also is a time for the team to discuss any questions or concerns they have. Are staff members receiving frequent complaints? Do they need clarity about a new exhibition? Is there a question about how to handle a particular situation? Are there new questions from visitors? If someone has learned the answer to a past question or any other useful information, this is a great time to share those details. When these discussions are held in a group setting, the entire group starts to feel like they are problem-solving together and are on the same team.

If your teams use radios for communication, using the same channel can allow teams to better serve visitors by sharing information in the moment. If a visitor has a question and an employee doesn't know the answer, the employee can turn to the rest of the team for assistance. Most teams have members with differing interests and expertise, so people can help and learn from one another. When there is a security concern or emergency situation, such as a visitor behaving oddly, a medical emergency, or a physical threat, they can share information quickly. Clear communication in these instances is essential.

Radio communication also can help with service as the team shares information about visitors. One colleague may ask another to further direct a group to the exhibition they are interested in, someone may share the name of a young visitor's stuffed animal so others can greet it by name, or a team member may share that a particular group is very interested in stories and information. Communicating like this on a regular basis fosters camaraderie and sets up easier communication in more difficult moments.

At the Chicago History Museum, the director of visitor services attends the security team's meeting in order to hear about visitor concerns and upcoming events. The two parties also communicate throughout the day about visitor concerns. If there is a delicate situation with a visitor, the security team can call the director of visitor services to come and assist. This is a prime example of using everyone's strengths for the betterment of the team.

## Cross-Training

One way to encourage teamwork is to cross-train key staff members from each department in multiple roles. This increases flexibility and can be particularly helpful in small and midsize museums where teams may be very small. If only one or two employees are assigned to a post at any given time, an employee calling out sick can cause a large disruption to operations. This problem can be exacerbated if no one else knows how to cover the sick employee's role. You want people to stay home when they are sick, but good employees often will come in anyway if they think they are leaving the institution in a bad spot. Cross-training your team allows for greater flexibility at the last minute. This also allows for flexibility in scheduling, allowing the supervisor to grant more requests for time off.

Visitor traffic patterns change throughout the day, so teams may be busy at different times. Cross-training allows teams to help one another and provide the best service to visitors. There may be a rush at the admission desk right before a scheduled program, in the museum store before a tour bus departs, or at a tour entrance as school groups arrive. If team members can easily flow between positions, the same number of staff members can cover a wider area.

In addition to the gains in flexibility, understanding other facets of the museum can help individual employees be more successful in their roles. If museum store associates have training in the galleries, they may learn more about the collection, allowing them to better sell the merchandise in the store. If people who work in ticketing spend time with security enforcing rules, they may change their orientation to incorporate an explanation of some rules. Having a broader knowledge of staff roles helps all employees have a more comprehensive view of the visitor experience.

When a museum trains its employees in multiple areas, the employees are likely to feel that the museum recognizes their hard work and is invested in them and their professional development. This additional training gives them a better understanding of museum operations and helps the team as a whole. Investment in staff development and growth also helps the museum retain strong performers.

## Training Together

Beyond cross-training to teach employees other people's jobs, consider bringing different departments together for their regular training sessions. There is a lot of information that is useful to multiple departments. For example, a detailed curator tour of a new exhibition is valuable to everyone, but people will use the information in different ways. A tour guide will create a tour specific to the local school curriculum, a gallery attendant will choose a few interesting facts to share with visitors, and a museum store associate will connect the information to the related merchandise. Learning these things together allows employees to form relationships with one another, fostering a true team atmosphere.

This same approach applies to other topics such as information about your visitors, your service standards, emergency procedures, and accessibility. Everyone can learn the information at the same time and then apply it to their own roles.

## Hybrid Training Models

Some museums have created hybrid training models that blend several traditional museum roles into one job. This could include grouping ticketing staff, theater ushers, and store associates under one umbrella. Doing this helps with cross-training and coverage during busy periods.

The North Carolina Museum of Art has absorbed retail operations into the visitor experience team. This move allows the museum to provide seamless service across all frontline operations. The team also can utilize both the retail and ticketing platforms in all locations, allowing visitors to purchase tickets, memberships, and merchandise as quickly and easily as possible.

One successful model combines security and service staff in the galleries. Prime examples of this model can be found at the Chrysler Museum of Art, the Denver Art Museum, and The Broad. This model does not take security any less seriously; the staff believe that one can be firm and kind at the same time. The focus on service provides a welcoming atmosphere and enhances the experience. This model is discussed further in the next chapter.

## THE IMPORTANCE OF LEADERSHIP

Leadership is important in every department throughout the museum, and the frontline team depend on their leaders for a wide range of support. In addition to the support and guidance that is necessary for all employees, employees in visitor-facing positions have more time-sensitive needs. Positions in visitor services, security, the museum store, and similar departments are based on consistent coverage, meaning that someone needs to be at each post at all times. This requires a bit more hands-on management, but it doesn't mean that employees need to be micromanaged. It means these employees need easy access to support and someone to check in on them throughout the day. Due to the coverage needs, someone needs to greet the employees as they arrive for the day, review the day's activities, and change assignments if a staff member has not arrived or activities have changed. Each break will need to be covered, and questions often require immediate answers. You can't appoint a single leader who works elsewhere in the museum and is disconnected from the visitor experience. That person will not be able to respond with the speed that the frontline team needs. The frontline team will need support from staff with more seniority throughout the museum.

There are a few types of leadership needed for frontline teams. Some larger teams may have additional layers of management and some smaller teams may combine roles, but in all situations, these needs will have to be met. Frontline staff need someone who is leading the team from the floor, a manager who provides planning and vision for the department, and someone who is an advocate for the team to the rest of the museum and the industry.

### From the Floor

When you have visitors in front of you, small problems can feel significantly more stressful. This is especially true if you don't feel like there is anyone around to help. Small stressors, such as an upset visitor, a software error, or a long line of visitors, can feel overwhelming on your own. The first level of support that frontline team members need is to simply feel like they have backup as they go about their jobs. This includes having someone to call when they have questions and who will cover them for a quick break, help them through busy periods, and respond to incidents.

Some frontline employees are so focused on excelling in their individual roles that they may not see beyond their own performance. For example, say you have four staff members working on two tasks, with two employees focused on each. One area gets a rush of visitors while the other remains slow. The simple solution is to move one employee from the slow area to the busy one and to stay divided three to one for as long as necessary. Some employees will be so focused on their own roles, they won't see this situation evolving. They also may not feel confident making the decision to reassign themselves or others.

These employees need someone who is readily available and is focused on everything happening in the public areas of the museum. Someone in a lead, senior-associate, or similar role is in a good position to lend this first layer of support. This person often is still actively working on the floor, at least a portion of the time, but also is assigning tasks, making changes throughout the day, assisting with complicated situations, covering breaks, and responding to small incidents.

If there is no one designated in this type of role, a few problems can occur. Team members may voluntarily step into the role and appoint themselves as the leaders. They will offer help to their colleagues, make decisions in the moment, and assign tasks. Sometimes this works out well and showcases the best people for the job. In that case, these individuals deserve recognition for the work they are doing and an official role. Other times, this self-appointment causes problems and leads to resentment among the team members. It can be difficult to be directed by a peer, particularly if there is disagreement about the best course of action.

There also can be times when a decision needs to be made, and no one is willing to make it. People may be afraid to step forward and be that team member who is resented. This can result in poor service, or worse, can waste valuable time in an emergency. You can avoid this problem by promoting someone from the frontline staff. If you are wondering who is ready, look for someone who recognizes the big picture beyond their own work, demonstrates excellent customer-service skills, and remains calm in emergencies.

## A Strong Manager Fosters a Strong Team

The team needs more than just consistent support on the floor. They also need a leader who supports each employee as an individual and manages the short- and long-term goals of the department.

First and foremost, a successful person in this role must have excellent customer-service skills. They will need to be a strong role model for their team, help coach individuals on their service skills, and coordinate service training for the team. They will be the one to handle complex visitor concerns. They decide when to approve exceptions to museum rules. For example, the museum may not allow visitors to carry backpacks, but they may make an exception for a teacher carrying medications on a field trip. A visitor services manager, or someone in a similar role, needs empathy to make the right decisions, being flexible where possible and firm where needed for safety. They should also be capable of finding an alternative solution when they do have to say no. In the backpack example, if it's not possible to allow the teacher to carry the backpack, the manager could loan the teacher a different type of bag to use during their visit.

This person needs to be skilled at handling complaints. They must be open to visitor feedback and approach each conversation as an opportunity to learn. They should make visitors feel heard and respected without causing the team to feel like they don't have support. To do this, they first need to get the visitor to a comfortable place if necessary. The next and most important step is to listen with empathy and allow the visitor to tell their entire story. They should not interrupt and should ask questions where appropriate. They can then apologize and explain any museum policies or misunderstandings. It's important to recognize that a team member may have made an error, but the manager should be careful not to jump to conclusions and assume the worst of their team. It is important to not be defensive or argumentative. That will not help the situation. Hopefully, the manager can find a solution that works for the visitor.

In addition to customer-service skills, this leader needs organizational skills including scheduling and budgeting. They also need to be strong in hiring, training, and developing employees. These topics are all discussed in future chapters.

In the section above, we talked about someone needing to see beyond his or her own performance to recognize the needs of the whole team. At the management level, someone must begin to see beyond the needs of their own department to understand what is best for the entire institution. There may be times when something may not be ideal for their department but is best for the institution. This could include closing a portion of the museum to the public, altering schedules, or assigning the team an undesirable task. A successful leader needs to recognize these occurrences and communicate about them in a positive way to the team.

This person also needs to be trusted by the institution and empowered to make decisions as necessary. They may need to refund money or offer complimentary items to make visitors happy, close galleries if needed, ask disruptive visitors to leave the museum, or take the lead in an emergency. They need guidance and support from the institution to accomplish these goals.

## Advocacy to Senior Staff

The frontline team also needs support from beyond their own department. They need people throughout the institution to recognize their needs, celebrate their successes, and make their work part of strategic plans and goals.

Hopefully, the frontline team has many advocates throughout the institution, but a key person for them is the senior staff member who oversees these forward-facing departments. This person should be chosen carefully. While they may or may not have direct work experience in this area, they should be passionate about the visitor experience. They should support the growth of the team members (particularly the department leaders), look for opportunities to showcase the team, and include the frontline team directly in planning whenever possible.

This person is likely to be involved in institutional strategic planning, trustee interactions, and senior staff meetings. They have a responsibility to represent the frontline team and your visitors in these situations. This person should regularly share the concerns and successes of the frontline team with other senior staff members so those leaders have an accurate understanding of what is happening on the floor. In the same vein, this person also should report back to the frontline team about discussions with other senior staff members. This allows the frontline team to gain a better understanding of the entire institution.

Advocates also will need to share strategic priorities and show the frontline team how their role fits in with those institutional goals. For example, if the museum has goals relating to diversity and accessibility, the frontline staff can share valuable feedback they have heard from visitors about these issues. If the museum is embarking on green initiatives, the frontline team can help with the implementation of the public-facing portions of the plans. In both cases, the frontline team also can share progress and contribute ideas over time.

Each museum will have a unique staffing structure to meet the needs of its visitors. No matter what the structure looks like, your frontline team must work together and have the support they need.

# 8

## Merging Security and Service

Museums are presented with two equally important tasks.

The first is the heavy responsibility of protecting the objects in our care and preserving them for future generations. Museum professionals take this very seriously and believe in the power and importance of these objects. At the same time, our missions stress the importance of not just locking these objects away but also sharing them with our community in a meaningful way. Too often, museum professionals think of these as two distinct tasks that can't overlap. They may believe that they can focus on only one or the other in a given moment. This usually results in one department providing security and another focusing on engagement. Visitors view the museum staff and volunteers as one team, no matter the organization chart. You should think of your team in the same way.

As you mapped your visitor experience in chapter 4, you listed the opportunities throughout the journey for visitors to interact with your employees. In many museums, these employees might include a security officer at the entrance, an admission representative, security officers throughout the galleries, and a sales associate in the museum store. Now is the time to ask if you have the right type of employees in the right positions to create the best experience.

### MULTIPLE WAYS TO ACHIEVE A SAFE ENVIRONMENT

Whether your security team is its own department, part of a larger hybrid department, or a third-party contractor, it is an important component of the visitor experience and has great influence on your visitors. While most museums are largely focused on the same security-related tasks, each museum approaches those tasks in different ways.

#### Traditional Model

A traditional museum-security team is designed to be an intimidating presence in the galleries. Officers are positioned around the perimeter of public spaces, often purposely removed from the experience, and are directed to avoid engaging with visitors.

I have worked on projects with traditional security teams at institutions beyond my own and there were a few things that were true with each team. Overall, the teams were composed of hardworking individuals who took the responsibility of their work seriously. When I inquired about objects that were frequently touched or rules that were frequently broken, I encountered a real hesitancy in each museum. There was a consistent fear among security teams that admitting rules were broken meant they had failed. The teams were genuinely concerned that they would somehow be in trouble or be blamed for these situations.

While they understood that rule enforcement was a critical part of their jobs, they were not given much direction or training regarding how to enforce those rules. When this is combined with the fear mentioned above, it can lead to overly stern enforcement. A security team may not see customer service as part of their role as they don't want to be seen as soft. When they observe a consistent problem, such as an item being touched frequently, they are not empowered to report it or be part of a solution.

Within the organization, they can feel disconnected from other museum departments as well. This places the security department in its own silo, finding its work distinct and not part of a larger mission. The team is narrowly focused on the task at hand and not empowered to collaborate or share their thoughts with others. Due to building design, they often are physically separate from other departments as well. This can lead to using language that references physical proximity, such as "upstairs versus downstairs staff." You want to do as much as you can to help your security team feel like a valued part of the overall team.

As a visitor, I toured a museum that was formerly a personal residence. I noticed a small room and asked a security officer what the original purpose was. Based on my experience, I felt it was very natural to ask questions of the people working in the galleries. This gentleman discreetly guided me to a corner of the room, away from his colleagues, and he was clearly hiding the fact that he was talking to me. He answered my question in a thoughtful and engaging way. It definitely added to my experience and helped me put the building in context. I wish he would have been able to share the story freely with other visitors.

Security officers in the traditional model can be set up to fail if we do not support them more. If this is the model you choose, you need to provide ample training, create clear lines of communication, and make sure the security team feels connected to the larger organization.

## A Fresh Approach

Several museums saw that the traditional security model either wasn't working for them or wouldn't work for them in their new museum. They moved away from this model in an effort to improve the visitor experience and increase the level of engagement in the galleries.

The Academy Museum of Motion Pictures, The Broad, the Chrysler Museum of Art, and the Denver Art Museum have all developed staff positions that address security needs and enhance the visitor experience. The people in these positions serve in a hybrid role that blends security, service, and engagement. These gallery hosts or visitor service associates are responsible for answering questions, monitoring visitor behavior, enforcing rules, and engaging visitors in conversation about the collections and exhibitions.

In practice, this means the same person may greet a visitor at the door, help the visitor through the ticketing process, and engage with the visitor in the galleries. One person could be in all those roles in a single day, and everyone working in those roles is part of the same larger team. In some models, this person's role may include providing guided educational tours or working in the museum store.

**Figure 8.1.** *Source: Chrysler Museum of Art*

In the galleries, each employee may be assigned to a stationary post or have a zone to cover with regular rounds. During one of these assignments, a staff member may answer a question about the history of the museum, ask a visitor not to touch something, point out something interesting about a work that can go unseen, and listen to a child's story about their dog who looks like the one in the picture. It becomes easy and natural to flow between these actions.

While this model increases the opportunities for engagement, it also acknowledges individual preferences. Some museum visitors want to explore on their own, and this model allows for that. When you focus not just on potential trouble but also on body language, tone of voice, and apparent interest, you can craft exceptional experiences tailored to each visitor.

### Security and Service: Is It Really Possible to Do Both?

Museums that have adopted this model are often asked about the safety of their collections. It's great to be friendlier, but does it really work? All these museums would answer with an emphatic yes! Many of these museums have several years of experience with this model, and no one would stick with it if they didn't truly think it was safe. This model is supported by the leadership teams, curators, registrars, and conservators. With this model, the firmness of rule enforcement and the vigilance of each team is not diminished. It is absolutely possible to be firm and polite at the same time. The keys are clear expectations, solid training, empowerment of the frontline staff, and communication from the frontline team to the rest of the museum.

As you hire individuals, you need to be sure that they have strengths in both service and security. Most service jobs include some sort of rule enforcement, so asking about experience with this can help you find the right people. In training, you need to spend time role-playing your style of rule enforcement. The more prepared staff members are for these conversations, the more natural those interactions will become. If staff appear nervous when enforcing a rule, it makes the situation more awkward for everyone. You also need to spend some time discussing visitor behavior. You'll be approaching this from a perspective of both service and security. Understanding your visitors' motivations, interests, and preferences can help you provide visitors with the best possible service.

You also need to discuss behavior that stands out and how to approach those situations. This includes operational questions that you will need to instruct your staff not to answer. Again, preparing for this ahead of time helps staff handle the situation smoothly in the moment. For example, if someone asks about the monetary value of an object, staff should be prepared to answer that the object is priceless, or that they don't know about the value but the object is one of their favorites.

In order to accommodate the preferences mentioned above, you will also spend time focused on engagement. You'll talk about how to approach visitors and give advice on easy ways to start conversations, such as sharing favorites or asking visitors for their thoughts. You also need to discuss how to remain vigilant with security duties while engaging with the public. This includes physically positioning oneself during a conversation where one can still see the whole room rather than solely looking directly at the display with the visitor. This is demonstrated in figure 8.2. If a visitor is too close to the object, the employee can take a step back from the individual while talking. The person will naturally step back too, adding distance between them and the object.

**Figure 8.2.   *Source: Chrysler Museum of Art***

Museums that have these hybrid employees in public areas also have strong, professional security teams behind the scenes. These teams often are watching the public areas on cameras and are ready to provide assistance with troublesome visitors or assist in an emergency. This provides separation while allowing the entire security team to be unified.

### Designing Your Own Security Model

You may find that none of the models listed above quite works for your museum. You may be interested in adding more engagement in your galleries but are not willing, or don't have the support, to completely replace the forward-facing security staff. You can design a hybrid model that works for your institution or take small steps toward your ultimate goal.

If you have two or more distinct departments that work in public areas, a great first step is to work on communication between these departments. This starts with the leaders of each department working together, openly discussing who should handle specific situations, and letting everyone's strengths shine. Your security team may call a leader from visitor services when there is a sensitive situation with a visitor because that employee is better equipped to have a challenging conversation. If a visitor is not listening to the ticketing staff, you want your security team to step in and help provide support.

Look for opportunities for these departments to train as one group. Training together reinforces the idea that everyone is part of one larger team and helps them build relationships that will be useful in their daily jobs and during any incidents. These training sessions could cover emergency procedures, accommodating visitors with disabilities, a new exhibition, the history of the museum, diversity and inclusion, or any topic that involves every department. You also can have team members lead training sessions for one another to share their expertise.

You could try adding staff focused on engagement while leaving some posts covered by your traditional security team. Special exhibitions or popular areas are good places to test this structure. You can then slowly add service associates throughout your museum or maintain a permanent combination with some posts staffed by each type of employee. You might place a security officer at the main entrance and pair additional security officers with service staff discussing engaging exhibitions in the most crowded areas.

The North Carolina Museum of Art has united all its frontline teams with its campus-host training program. This program connects new staff to tools and more experienced staff members who share the museum's mission, and it stresses everyone's role on campus in creating a welcoming experience for all visitors. Knowing the campus, art, and where to find answers is imperative. Staff also greet visitors whenever they see visitors in the galleries or park. The visitor experience is a shared responsibility.

## COLLABORATION AND COMMUNICATION

No matter how you structure your service and security staff, whether as one team or multiple, security is a critical function of the visitor experience, and to some degree, security is a responsibility of every museum staff member. Communication is imperative to achieve an environment that protects visitors, staff, and the collection.

The employees on the floor need a way to communicate in real time with one another, their supervisors, and employees watching surveillance cameras. Portable radios are generally a good solution for this that works in most museums. If there is an emergency or there is a visitor who is exhibiting odd behavior, you want to be able to share that information quickly and discreetly.

Earpieces are essential for keeping the conversation private. For example, say a security officer watching the cameras wants to share that the little girl in the red dress is touching objects as soon as the gallery staff member leaves the room. This is an important message to convey, but you do not want your visitors to overhear it. If a visitor is behaving oddly, you want all employees to know that, but you don't want any visitors, particularly the visitor in question, to overhear that conversation. This communication allows behind-the-scenes staff to follow such visitors on camera while frontline staff are mindful in the galleries. If the situations escalate, everyone can act quickly. If nothing comes of them, then no one's visit was spoiled.

If there is an incident, large or small, the frontline staff needs to have clear lines of communication to the right individuals after the fact. Visitor injuries or other incidents should be reported to the leadership team as well as managers of security and facilities. Such communication makes the executive director aware of the situation so they can better respond if they get a phone call about it. The facilities manager may want to look at the location of an injury to be sure there isn't an obstacle that should be repaired. If incidents happen in a repeated location or manner, many people may want to work together to see how future incidents can be prevented.

For incidents that involve potential damage to the collection, your team should be able to quickly send a report to leadership, conservation, registration, and the curator of that content area. Damage could be something small like a pencil mark or rough touch, or something more serious like visible damage. In serious situations, the frontline manager should feel comfortable calling these individuals, even after hours or on the weekends. If the same object is included in several of these reports, the groups can discuss solutions such as adding a barrier, covering the object with a vitrine, or moving the object to another location.

Collaboration between departments will be discussed further in chapter 12.

## KEY COMPONENTS OF SECURITY

Security duties can generally be divided into two categories: behind-the-scenes responsibilities and public-facing duties. Here we are addressing those tasks that are essential in public spaces. Each of these duties is necessary but can be achieved by people in a variety of roles. When security tasks include interacting with visitors, they must be approached with both safety and service in mind.

### Visitor Safety

When someone is a guest in your home, you want that person to feel safe, comfortable, and welcome. The same applies to visitors at your museum. Clearly, you need to design a safe environment that is free from obstructions, trip hazards, standing water, and hazardous materials, but you also want the environment to be safe from harassment and the team to be prepared to help visitors in an emergency.

#### Safe Space for Everyone

Museums are spaces where we can listen to varying perspectives, discover something new, and learn about our individual and collective cultural history. This necessitates an open-minded environment that is truly a community resource. There is absolutely no room for racism, bigotry, or harassment.

It is the role of the public-facing staff members and supervisors to ensure this safe environment. Your human resources department has likely done a good job of addressing how staff members need to interact with one another. You need to be clear with your team about how this respect extends into the galleries. First, you need to be clear about how you want employees to treat visitors. Visitors are diverse and there can be no tolerance for any disrespect. This is probably the most expected portion of this discussion. Very few service workers feel they can harass customers.

The other scenarios, a visitor harassing an employee or a visitor harassing another visitor, also need to be clearly addressed with your team in their training. Unfortunately, many frontline employees may feel they need to accept inappropriate behavior from visitors. This is likely a result of bad policies at their former employers. You need to be clear that this is not acceptable and tell them how they should handle various situations in which visitors are behaving inappropriately.

If someone makes a staff member uncomfortable in any way, the staff member needs to know that they should call the supervisor, and the supervisor will remove the employee from the situation immediately. This could apply to situations in which a visitor is simply talking too much to a specific employee or a visitor is romantically interested in a staff member. The supervisor's response can be as simple as swapping the employee with a different one or the supervisor staying in the area. The troublesome visitor could be a first-time visitor, a frequent attendee, or someone the employee knows from outside the museum. If it is a repeated situation, you want to be sure that everyone is aware and prepared to act.

When visitors are behaving inappropriately toward other visitors, the institution must step in. Whenever possible, this should be handled by a supervisor, but your frontline staff members need to understand that racist or bigoted comments, microaggressions, harassing behavior, or threats of violence will not be tolerated. For overheard comments, you may be able to start with a firm statement that the museum is a welcoming place for everyone, and that kind of behavior or language is not acceptable. Depending on the nature of the event, the individual may be asked to leave the museum.

Situations like these can escalate quickly, so you also need to have clear lines of communication with your team and other departments. You need to devise clear codes that everyone knows and understands. Make sure these codes differentiate between a visitor you want everyone to keep an eye on and someone who may become violent. If someone feels threatened, you want that information to travel as quickly as possible.

In any stressful situation, you want your team to have some de-escalation skills in order to prevent situations from getting worse. The Denver Art Museum includes de-escalation skills in their staff training to mitigate situations that occur and help their staff feel prepared for these circumstances.

### *Emergency Preparedness*

When an emergency happens, you need employees to remain calm, remember and execute the correct procedures, and prioritize the comfort and safety of visitors. These situations could include a visitor injury, a missing child, potential damage to your collection, evacuating the building due to a fire alarm, and much more. Both service and security staff can be trained to handle these situations effectively. In many museums, these teams need to work together in an emergency, so emergency preparedness is a great opportunity for cross-training and collaboration.

You need to design and test procedures for each of these situations. As you practice, you need to include all public-facing departments and anyone else who has a role in an emergency. After each drill or actual emergency, you should have open discussions about what went right and wrong. Be open to ideas for improvement from your team. Your staff understand visitors' movements and can provide valuable insight. You also can look for ways to collaborate and discuss those ideas with the team. For example, does one department have more staff on the weekends than another? Could the teams blend or share duties in these procedures to make it easier on everyone? Does one group find a particular task challenging? Could the task be shared?

As you design your procedures, you want clear processes, but there needs to be flexibility built in as well. If someone can't remember a code for an injury, you want that person to use plain language and say that a visitor has fallen. The person also needs to communicate the severity of the situation if additional equipment, such as an automated external defibrillator (AED), is needed. Everyone needs to know this information immediately.

Avoid plans that are too regimented regarding who alerts your security team or who calls emergency services. If a front-of-house manager is the only person who can call for security, what happens if the manager is the one involved in the incident? If only one person is authorized to call the emergency number, what about the delay of reaching that person? Flexibility helps facilitate a speedy response.

In addition to the critical nature of handling the emergency directly, employees need to be alert, keep security at the forefront of their minds, and remain vigilant. They need to be sure that the emergency is not designed to distract the employees from something else. For example, they need to know that someone is not faking a medical emergency or pulling a fire alarm to draw employees away from some other activity. It is human nature to want to help in these situations, so it will take practice for employees to stay on task. In the moment, a supervisor needs to make sure all areas are covered (at least one person will have been pulled away to address the situation) and remind staff to stay alert in their assigned posts.

Once the emergency is under control for the moment, it's time to consider visitor comfort. If a visitor requires first aid, that's the top priority, but once that is being tended to, someone else can set up a barrier to keep other visitors away and allow for privacy. If you need to evacuate the building, someone should wait with the visitors outside to reassure them.

In addition to the training you provide for everyone regarding emergencies and incidents of visitor behavior, you need to provide supervisors and managers with further thorough training. These leaders' demeanor will guide the situation, so they need to remain calm and confident. You want to discuss the nuances of various situations and what you may do, who to involve, and how they should use their own judgment.

For example, discuss the following questions regarding visitor injuries: What should they do if someone refuses care in a variety of situations? When a situation occurs in public spaces, how can they close off various rooms or areas from the public? If someone needs CPR, how can they provide as much privacy as possible when the person's chest is exposed?

Discuss these questions regarding evacuations: How will staff accommodate someone who can't use the stairs since elevators should not be used in case of fire? Where could someone hide to avoid evacuation, and how can you be sure that area is checked? What if someone refuses to leave the restaurant because they just got their food?

Go into this same level of detail with each type of emergency.

## Presence

A traditional security officer is designed to be intimidating through their posture, their uniform design, and the style of their interactions. This intimidation has its place, but is it the only impression or experience you want to provide visitors in your galleries?

With a traditional security presence, visitors receive the message that the employees know they are there and are watching their behavior. This can be an important deterrent to inappropriate behavior. While some sort of deterrent is essential for most museums, it can also send a message that visitors are not trusted, they are being followed, and their behavior is being judged.

You can achieve a presence that deters negative behavior without alienating your visitors. If you add a genuine, warm greeting and an offer to answer questions, the message is now that the employees know visitors are there, visitors are welcome here, and security can see visitors' behavior. This approach is still a deterrent, but the message is strikingly different. Consider which presence you want in your museum.

### Visual Impression

Your employees set the tone in the galleries and that starts with their uniform. Traditionally, security has worn a very formal uniform, something such as a classic blue blazer with gold buttons. That may be the right choice for some museums, but you should think about the message you want to send and match uniforms to that goal.

If you want visitors to feel relaxed and comfortable, then that should be reflected in staff apparel. Visitor service associates at The Broad wear all black with red lanyards. Gallery hosts at the Chrysler Museum of Art wear warm blue sweaters or polo shirts. Each museum chose a uniform that matches its community, looks professional, makes the employees easy to spot, and is part of an overall warm greeting.

**Figure 8.3.** *Source: Chrysler Museum of Art*

A change in uniform should be a part of an institutional change, not simply a change of clothes. It's not enough to put employees in casual uniforms and give them a button that says "ask me" or "I'm happy to help." This only works if you have hired people who genuinely want to help, trained them to offer a warm welcome, and empowered them to provide a genuine, engaging experience.

In addition to the staff uniform, body language is an important part of the visual impression for visitors. Whether your team members are stationary or are making rounds to cover an assigned zone, their body language should be open and welcoming. They should avoid placing their hands on their hips or crossing their arms, and their phones should stay in their pockets. They need to be conscious that they are not blocking the path of visitors and of course aren't looking visitors up and down, snickering or laughing at visitors, looking judgmental, or acting impatient. A simple training exercise to help with this is to have the team stand up and mimic what they think judgmental, impatient, snotty, or intimidating behavior looks like. As a group they will enjoy laughing together and hopefully be more aware of their own behavior. Referencing this exercise also helps managers if they need to have follow-up coaching conversations to correct behavior.

## Observation

It's important that your visitors see employees in the galleries, but it's even more important that the employees are observing your visitors. Observing visitor behavior can help you reach both your security and your service goals.

Visitors are unique and will move through your museum in different ways. You need to work with your team to be sure they welcome those differences, adjust their service for each individual, and make note of any security concerns.

Experienced frontline staff understand the natural flow of visitors and notice when something is off. Are visitors dressed oddly for the weather? Are they moving at an unusual speed? Are they focusing on operations (cameras, doors, staff rotations) rather than the works on display? What are they taking photographs of? What type of questions are they asking? Your staff should be wary of questions about the number of staff, locations of security cameras, object value, how exhibitions move in and out of the museum, and anything else too operational.

It's important that employees in your public spaces are alert to visitor behavior, notice these exceptions, and communicate these to their colleagues. While these behaviors should be noted, you also need to be cautious not to jump to conclusions too quickly or exclude someone based on one mildly unusual action. Visitors are allowed to be unique and behave in unexpected ways. Someone may be asking a lot of questions about the specifics of a museum job because she is trying to map employee patterns, or because she is interested in a museum career. Someone making unusual noises or moving quickly could have a disability and simply be moving at their own pace. You want to be both alert and respectful.

When you do see visitors exhibiting odd behavior, you may find that engagement is your strongest tool. Rather than following visitors and accusing them of doing something nefarious, you can welcome them, ask them about their visits, and talk to them about their museum interests. If someone is just a little different from your average visitor, you have helped enhance the person's visit. If that person was considering something inappropriate, this can be a deterrent. Either way, you send a strong but overall positive message.

An advantage to having service staff in the galleries is that beyond observing and looking for unusual behavior, these employees can observe and respond to visitors who look lost, intimidated, confused, or inquisitive. The staff can then offer help and move the experience in a positive direction. If people are lost, ask if you can help them find anything. If people look a little intimidated, a warm greeting and a fun fact about the object they are looking at can help them relax and enjoy their visits. Can you answer any questions they have about the work, or can you tell them how to learn more? These small gestures can make a big impact, and observing your visitors can help you implement those ideas at just the right time.

## Rule Enforcement

Museum rules are important, but the truth is that visitors will break your rules at times. This is unavoidable, and what happens next can make or break the experience for the visitor. As mentioned in chapter 2, a previous negative experience is one of the reasons that people don't visit museums. Unfortunately, many of these interactions are with security officers and revolve either around feeling followed through the museum or around rule enforcement.

Museum rules seem obvious to museum staff and experienced museumgoers, but they may seem arbitrary or surprising to novice visitors. As museums seek to attract new audiences, we must examine how we enforce our rules because this is frequently reported as a pain point, particularly for newer visitors.

We have all tried new experiences in which we might not know the formal policies or etiquette. We may be comfortable visiting a museum but might make mistakes the first time we attend a stock-car race, a wine tasting, or a Renaissance fair. In those cases, we would hope that someone wouldn't yell at us from a distance, belittle us for not knowing the rule, and then follow us to be sure that it didn't happen again. The opposite approach would be to come from a place of education rather than embarrassment or bullying. A staff member could approach the individual, explain the rule at a normal volume, and maintain an understanding tone. The former implies the idea that the visitor doesn't belong, while the latter shows that they can belong; they just need to learn a few new things.

The Broad uses the "authority of the resource" method of rule enforcement. This technique was developed by the National Park Service and puts the focus on the object that is being protected.[1] It stresses the importance of the object and asks for the visitor's help preserving and protecting the object, rather than focusing on the fact that a rule was broken. An example may be stating that you notice a visitor touching the work, and while you understand the temptation, the object can be damaged by the oils in the person's hands. Ask for the visitor's help moving forward in order to protect the object.

The Chrysler Museum of Art follows a five-point method of rule enforcement that focuses on not embarrassing the visitor, approaching the visitor, speaking at a normal volume, explaining the reason behind the rule, and, most importantly, stressing that the correction isn't the end of the interaction. After the rule is explained, that's a great moment to add a fun fact or short story about the work of art.

As you look at your philosophy around rule enforcement, take a moment to consider if all your rules are necessary. Sometimes old rules are still on the books, simply because they always have been. These could include things that have a negative impact on the visitor experience. For example, rules around photography have changed greatly over the past several years. People are so used to photographing their daily activities that you should allow photography wherever possible. You may need to adjust your rules as technology and trends change, such as adding language about selfie sticks. You don't want your employees spending so much of their time focused on enforcing unnecessary rules that they don't have time to watch overall behavior and engage with visitors.

There is a large difference between someone who makes an innocent mistake and someone who deliberately continues to break rules. Visitors who do not correct their behavior need to be reminded and, if necessary, referred to a manager who can reiterate the importance of the rules. Visitors who don't comply at that point or who are abusive to staff regarding rule enforcement should be asked to leave the museum. Starting with a warmer approach does not mean that you can't be firm. As mentioned above, it's very possible to be firm and polite at the same time.

No matter how you organize your staff, your success relies on the strength of your team. If you want to keep the best employees happy and fulfilled, you need to recognize their skills, show them respect, and treat them as true professionals.

## NOTE

1. *Interpretive Solutions: Harnessing the Power of Interpretation to Help Resolve Critical Resource Issues: Natural Resource Report NPS/NRPC/NRR—2011/290*, U.S. Department of the Interior, http://npshistory.com/publications/interpretation/nrr-2011-290.pdf

# 9

## Hiring Your Dream Team

There is absolutely nothing that has a greater impact on the experience of your visitors than the quality of your frontline team. This is true beyond museums and is evident in most service industries. As people tell stories about their favorite experiences, there often is a friendly employee featured as a key component. This could be the bartender who helped create your new favorite drink, the diver who helped you conquer your snorkeling fear so you could swim with sea turtles, or the tennis instructor who helped you nail your serve. People make a difference and elevate experiences from good to great.

### IDENTIFYING WHAT YOU ARE LOOKING FOR

The first task is to outline what you are looking for in a new team member. Which traits are most important to you? Who are your visitors and how could your employees best welcome them? What are your service principles and who will help you implement them?

### The Wrong Traits to Focus On

There are some traits that inexperienced managers focus on that don't get you the team you really need. Those traits are largely based on the ease of training or scheduling for the manager rather than on long-term growth of the visitor experience.

#### *Familiarity with Ticketing Software*

The software solutions that are most commonly used by museums are relatively easy to use, and the basic ticket-selling functions can be taught quickly. Managers may be excited to hear that someone is familiar with their system and see this as an opportunity to expedite training, but this experience should not be a driving force in hiring. First, hiring someone with the wrong personality to save a few hours on training, no matter how short-staffed you are, is a decision you will regret. Also, you may use the system differently from the candidate's previous employer, so the person may actually make more errors if they default to old habits. You will still have to execute your full software training.

### Perceived Longevity

It's happened to every manager. You select an employee with great potential, devote time and energy to their training, and just as they are beginning to stand on their own, they resign, leaving you to start the process all over again. As frustrating as this may be, we have to accept that this is part of management and resist the urge to try too hard to prevent it in the future. Stephanie Wood from the Denver Museum of Nature and Science has a saying: "I hired you because you are young, smart, and ambitious and you will leave us because you are young, smart, and ambitious." Frontline positions often have a higher turnover, and that turnover is bound to increase as you select higher quality candidates, but the turnover is worth it to have a consistently great team.

In one example from the Chrysler Museum of Art, a woman applied for a part-time gallery host position as she was completing her PhD program. The job worked with her schedule as she planned to spend the upcoming year working on her dissertation. I knew she would likely move on once she completed her degree, and some people questioned why I would hire her for what might be only a one-year tenure. I decided to hire her anyway, and I'm glad I did. If I had listened to their concerns, I would have missed out on a great employee. She was full of energy, a great teammate, an engaging storyteller, and she taught the rest of the team about nineteenth-century French history. She resigned for a teaching position at a local private school, and she now uses the museum's collection in her lessons, brings her students in for assignments whenever possible, and brings foreign students to visit regularly. She made a great impact on the team during her time with us and she still feels connected to the museum. This connection helps her continue to share the collection with others.

### Formal Education

Many candidates may have completed or be working toward degrees in history, art, biology, or other fields related to your museum. While there is no doubt that these individuals can contribute to your museum, be wary of hiring so many individuals with related degrees that it becomes a prerequisite. Your visitors will come with a variety of education levels, and your staff should as well. Formal education can absolutely be an asset to a candidate, but it is not the only way to gain knowledge or passion. Museums need to be sure they are communicating in a way that is as inclusive as possible, and having staff members with varied levels of education can help with this goal.

### Availability

Schedules for frontline teams can be complicated, and it's tempting to request that staff members have open availability. However, some of the most dynamic candidates may have education commitments, family obligations, or other employment. The best managers should be willing to juggle challenging scheduling needs in order to have the best team. Doing this will be a little more difficult for the manager but better for the visitor experience.

This does not mean that you shouldn't ask about availability and make sure candidates' availability fits with your needs. You need to cover all your operating hours, and you may need to make requirements for the team such as a minimum number of weekend days or evenings available. You should be as flexible as possible while still covering your assignments.

## Interview Skills

The candidates for your frontline positions may not have much experience with the interview process. They may not be polished in their wardrobe or confident in their answers, and their nerves may show. Do your best to look past these factors and try to learn about the candidate.

The candidate may have anxiety about what to wear and may choose what they consider the dressier items from their closet. They might choose a dress that is more of a sundress than a business dress or a shiny top more suitable for a night out than an interview. You may have seen interns make these same errors as they learn about business and business-casual dress. The business environment may be new to these interviewees, so try not to put too much weight on this factor, particularly if they will be wearing a uniform. If they show concerning judgment about professionalism in other ways during the interview, then this may be a concern. However, if they simply have worked in only casual environments, you should look past this.

As you conduct interviews, you may find a wide array of polish between applicants. This doesn't mean you shouldn't give proper credit to those who carry themselves well; you just want to keep an open mind for those who may not and look at the content of their answers.

## The Right Traits to Focus On

While there are some unique traits that you may look for when filling specific positions, there are several traits that are valuable in any frontline team member.

### Approachability and Attitude toward Service

You are hoping to find staff members who will make your visitors comfortable in your museum. Can those individuals provide a warm greeting and immediately put your visitors at ease? Do they enjoy talking to strangers? Will they strive to make visitors feel welcome in the museum the same way that a host or hostess might want people to feel in his or her home? This warmth and friendliness can be refined or improved with training, but it can't be created if absent. This friendliness is a core personality trait that shines through in a wide variety of people and is usually evident when you meet someone.

This same trait presents with a desire to help others have a great experience. It's not enough to want to chat with people. The standout candidates want to help everyone have the best individual experiences for themselves. To stress the importance of service, the North Carolina Museum of Art is focused on finding individuals who can give examples of how they serve their communities, and this is something they focus on in their interviews.

### Diversity

You've learned a lot about your visitors and your community. That knowledge should guide your hiring process. This means looking for a team that is diverse in ethnicity, age, education, socioeconomic background, primary language, parental status, and more. Unfortunately, not everyone has always felt welcome in museums. If your visitors see themselves reflected in your frontline team, it's a great step toward helping them feel like they belong. Individuals on your team also can learn from one another when their backgrounds are varied in every way.

Museums often talk about the need for more diversity in the field. This is another reason why the diversity of the frontline team is so important. For many museum professionals, their first job in a museum may be in visitor services or a similar department. If this is where employees will be promoted from, it's especially important that the team be diverse. As we look to attract young people to the field, allowing those people to see others like themselves when they visit museums may help them consider museum work as a possible career.

### *Empathy*

No matter how diverse your team is, your audience will always be more diverse, simply due to the number of visitors versus employees. It's important that your staff be able to relate to people who are different from them. Your staff may be very comfortable in museums, but they need to acknowledge that not all visitors will be. They may love talking with people in the galleries, but some visitors want to visit alone. They need to recognize that everyone will have different abilities, preferences, backgrounds, and knowledge levels and be able to adapt their service to individual visitors.

### *Judgment*

You will not be able to tell your new staff members exactly what to do in every possible situation. You are looking for individuals with good judgment who will combine their instincts with your training to make good decisions. Throughout the hiring process, candidates will not know your procedures, so your goal is simply to see what their instincts are. Do they want to help people? Do they lean toward being flexible to make visitors happy or stick strictly to the rules, and which approach lines up with your priorities?

### *Passion*

Individuals who are looking for a job working in service have many options to choose from. Museums have an advantage over other organizations since many candidates are passionate about what museums do. This doesn't always equate with formal study or a career path in the museum industry, but those candidates still believe in your mission. Do they think museums are awesome? Do they love the animals in your care? Do their faces light up when they talk about the history you are sharing? We all need a job for the paycheck, but are they excited about this job compared to other service positions?

## JOB-POSTING AND APPLICATION PROCESS

### Job Description

Once you've identified the traits you are looking for, you need to make sure those traits are reflected in the job description. The description should be straightforward and be clear about what the job entails. What are the main tasks of the position? Have you updated the description as the job has changed over time?

The Academy Museum of Motion Pictures includes in its job description, "You'll be a great candidate for this position if you . . ." and "This job might not be for you if . . ." For the visitor services associate position, managers are looking for people who are enthusiastic and friendly and like talking to people. They also mention that the work environment is noisy as that may not be desirable to all applicants. Other positions in the museum might involve working independently and not interacting often with others, which also is important to make clear to candidates.

Managers also carefully consider some skills that have been boilerplates on many job descriptions for similar positions. Are each of those skills necessary? Are the descriptions excluding candidates who may be excellent at the job? For example, does everyone need to be able to lift thirty pounds? Or is that task rare enough that it's ok if only a portion of the team can complete the task? If new boxes of brochures are unloaded once per week, you probably don't need every individual to have that ability.

The Academy Museum also uses software to evaluate its job descriptions for reading level (to be sure there isn't too much jargon), gender bias, and bias against candidates with disabilities. Managers want to be sure that they aren't just talking about diversifying the team and are doing all they can to help the museum reach that goal. They want this to be clear in their materials. Everyone is sincerely invited to apply; it is not just lip service.

### Job Posting

Where you post your job openings will impact who applies. Some museums may get great results from posting the job on their own websites or social media channels. Others get a stronger response from local or national job-posting websites. Each museum should try several options and note which applicants are more likely to use which methods. For example, is there a great spot to reach students? What if you are trying to reach older applicants? Where do you find the most diverse pool of applicants? No matter where you choose to post the position, be transparent about what you are looking for, what the job entails, and the rate of pay.

For the application process, some museums have their own online applications and others ask for a résumé and cover letter to be emailed directly to a hiring manager. The items you ask candidates to submit send a message about the type of position people are applying for. Asking for a résumé sends the message that you are hiring for a professional position, which may be seen differently from the application processes for other service jobs candidates may be considering. Being asked to submit a résumé helps candidates take this position seriously.

A custom application can allow you to ask specific questions and really zero in on specific traits you are looking for. You could ask why candidates are interested in this position, what they like about museums, or something else specific to your institution. Some museums may ask for additional documents with the application. For example, The Broad asks candidates to include videos of themselves enforcing a rule. Since this is a primary duty of the visitor services associate position, managers feel they get a true glimpse of how each individual would perform on the job. They also see candidates' abilities with technology, which they also believe are important to the position.

## INTERVIEWS

Hopefully you have a large pool of diverse applicants to choose from as you proceed to the interview stage. As you meet with your candidates, have the traits you are looking for at the forefront of your mind. Are candidates demonstrating passion for what you do? Does it look like they enjoy service? What did they choose to focus on in their introductions or cover letters? Do their personalities shine through? If you find that you can't always see this in the résumé or application, consider adding a brief phone screening in order to include a larger pool of applicants in the next stage. During that call, you can get a feel for candidates' personalities, ask any clarifying questions about their résumés or applications, make sure they understand the duties of the job, and ask one or two questions that are important to you.

The goal of an interview is to get a genuine impression of your candidates in a short time. The more comfortable and prepared your candidates are, the more likely you are to see their true personalities. As you call or set up interviews, give the candidates all the information you think they may need. What should they bring with them to the interviews? Where should they park? Which entrance should they come through? Is there anything they should be prepared for? You could tell them this directly, send an email before the interview, or simply have this information available on your website and let the applicants know where to find it.

The Academy Museum created an interview guide that is available to all candidates and discusses what candidates should think about wearing, where to park (specifying that the museum will pay for parking), and some questions candidates should be prepared to discuss. Managers don't want the interviews to feel like any kind of a "gotcha" or surprise moment.

### Interview Environment

As mentioned above, many candidates for frontline positions are not experienced with interviews. Be cognizant of their nerves and strive to make the environment as comfortable as possible. This way, you meet the genuine candidates and can truly see if they are a good fit for the position.

Start with the space where you will conduct the interview. Will it be comfortable for the candidates? Avoid a room that is too hot or too cold. Make sure you have a chair for candidates that will be comfortable for people of all sizes, doesn't squeak, and allows them to sit comfortably. Think about what you and any other interviewers are wearing. Choose something that projects the right tone and doesn't make candidates feel intimidated or feel foolishly overdressed. Have water available and a designated place for them to place their coats and bags. These small things may not faze seasoned interviewees, but they can really help less-experienced candidates feel more at ease.

### Getting Off to a Good Start

In order to combat the nervousness of your candidates, you should plan to do the talking first. Tell them about the position, the museum, and the team they would be part of. If you are trying to figure out how long to speak, one thing to look for is a bit of relaxation in the candidates' shoulders. Keep going until you see that; then it's a good time to encourage them to start talking. Begin with some background questions about their previous experience. These are questions they should be comfortable with, but inexperienced candidates may have very brief answers due to their nerves. Feel free to ask follow-up questions to encourage them and help them gain confidence. For example, if the candidate quickly replies that she was a hostess at a restaurant, and that's all she says, you can try to keep the conversation going. You can mention something you experienced at the restaurant, ask if she was busy during the recent citywide restaurant week, or ask what she liked about the job. Hopefully she will relax and expand more as the interview progresses.

**Types of Interview Questions**

Some of your questions will be focused on your service principles. It can be beneficial to just get your candidates talking about customer service in general, outside of museums. By doing this, you can see what they think good and bad service looks like. Does it come easily to them? Do their definitions line up with yours?

You also will ask questions that pull from candidates' previous work experience. Hearing how they have handled situations in the past will give you a good idea of how they would handle visitors at your museum. Can you see them in that role? If you have candidates with very little work experience, they may struggle to think of examples from their past and may look a little panicked. It can be helpful to have backup questions, moving from asking them for experiences to asking what they would do in particular situations that show the same skills you are trying to assess.

Situational questions like these can level the playing field and allow you to focus on real situations that occur at your museum. Candidates will not know your procedures so the answers may not be exactly what you would train them to do, but their answers will show you what their instincts are, and that is incredibly valuable.

**Sample Interview Questions**

*Skill: Problem-Solving*

Give us an example of a challenging situation you encountered at work and how you handled it.
    How would the solution work at your institution? Was the solution creative? Did the candidate put the customer first?

What would you do if a visitor asked you a question you didn't know the answer to?

> Bad Answer: "I would never admit I didn't know. I would make up an answer."
> Good Answer: "I would say I didn't know."
> Better Answer: "I would say I didn't know but I would try to find out."

What would you do if a visitor came to you with a ticket for the wrong IMAX movie time?

> Bad Answer: "I would tell them they got it wrong and there was no way to change it."
> Good Answer: "I would politely tell them it was the wrong time and send them to the front desk to get a new ticket."
> Better Answer: "I would check to see if there was any availability now, and I would work with the front desk to make the change later so the visitor isn't delayed getting to the movie."

*Skill: Empathy*

What would you say if a visitor was frustrated because they got lost on their way to the museum?

> Bad Answer: "I would tell them they should have googled it before they came."
> Good Answer: "I would commiserate. I still get lost around here too."
> Better Answer: "I would commiserate and say it can be confusing around here. I would tell the visitor that before leaving, they can stop by the desk and we'll print directions to make sure the visitor gets back safely."

A visitor asks what might be considered a silly question. Is the *Mona Lisa* here? Were dinosaurs real? How long can these fish breathe out of the water?

> Bad Answer: "I'd laugh at the visitor."
> Good Answer: "I'd answer matter-of-factly with no judgment."
> Better Answer: "I'd answer matter-of-factly with no judgment and then offer an additional fun fact about the topic."

### Skill: Service

How would you define good customer service? Can you give us examples of times when you received good and bad service as a customer?

The answer gives you an idea of the candidate's thoughts on service. Do those service principles line up with yours? Does the candidate struggle to think of positive examples but easily thinks of negative ones? Do you see other signs of negativity throughout the interview or is this just a single event?

Can you give us an example of a time you provided excellent customer service?

This should be a chance to see the candidate in the role he or she is interviewing for.

What would you say to a visitor who arrived at the museum thirty minutes before closing?

> Bad Answer: "I would turn the visitor away and say to come back tomorrow."
> Good Answer: "I'd welcome the visitor but say that we close in thirty minutes."
> Better Answer: "I'd welcome the visitor and say that we close in thirty minutes. I'd ask if the visitor is looking for anything in particular or make a suggestion of something that can be enjoyed in that time."

### Skill: Rule Enforcement

What would you say if you saw someone touching a work of art where touching was prohibited?

> Bad Answer: "I would yell and make sure the person stopped. Then I would follow the person closely to be sure it didn't happen again."
> Good Answer: "I would politely ask the person to stop."
> Better Answer: "I would politely ask the person to stop. Then I would explain the reason for the rule or say something interesting about the object the person was touching."

Can you give us an example of a time you had to enforce a rule?

Is the candidate comfortable in this role? Did the candidate try to embarrass the customer? Did the candidate explain the reason for the rule? Can you picture the candidate enforcing your rules in the manner that you require?

### Concluding the Interview

As you wrap up the interview, close with at least one question that gives people the chance to sell themselves one more time, such as why they are a good fit for the position. This gives them the chance to say anything they want to add that hasn't come up yet.

Give them an opportunity to ask questions and cover any topics that have not been discussed during the interview, particularly things they may not be sure if they should ask. They may want to ask questions like these: What is the rate of pay? What is the uniform and what portion is provided (e.g., if a red shirt is provided and people wear their own black pants)? What type of training is provided? What does a typical schedule look like? These questions may seem straightforward to you but can be very stressful and cause worry for candidates.

Be transparent about the hiring process and when candidates will hear from you. Give them a point of contact they can call or email if they have follow-up questions.

## SELECTING YOUR NEW TEAM MEMBERS

Once you have concluded your interviews, it's time to choose your new colleagues. Some museums choose to hire on a rolling basis, hiring throughout the year. This allows them to advertise constantly and not miss out on potential talent. Others choose to hire only a few times per year, which allows them to bring in a larger class for training. Your process will depend on the size of your team and your turnover rate.

Look at your current team. The best teams are diverse in many ways, so you don't always want to select only candidates who are similar to your current employees. You don't need a team of clones. In addition to ethnicity, age, and other demographic factors, think about personalities and how they relate to your visitors. Do you have a lot of highly energetic, bubbly types? Maybe it's time to balance with a few laid-back team members. What about their areas of passion and expertise? Which of your candidates can add something new? Is everyone on your current team young? Do you need some team members who are older or have children? Consider any characteristics that might help balance your current team.

Review your interview notes; who can you see in your museum? Who can relate to people who aren't like them? Who showed good decision-making skills? Who is passionate about your institution? Be a little wary of people who are passionate but don't seem interested in providing service. They may be interested in a museum career but a different position. It's wonderful to hire people who want to eventually work in other departments, but be sure they don't feel like they should already be in those roles. It can be clear when people feel the job is below them. If you do hire people with this mindset, it can bring the team down quickly.

Ultimately, the key thing to look for is personality. This cannot be covered by any specific interview question but shows throughout the entire conversation. Are candidates approachable and friendly? Would they provide your visitors with a warm welcome? Would they put people at ease? Can they add something to the visitor experience?

Overall, you should hire the personality. You can train the skill.

# 10

## Training to Develop a Dynamic Service Team

Training is everything. The peach was once a bitter almond; cauliflower is nothing but cabbage with a college education.

—Mark Twain

Hopefully you've assembled a great frontline team, but a well-conceived training program will help maximize the performance of each individual and the team as a whole. This chapter will help you outline your own training program based on the vision you have for service at your institution. While there are some specifics mentioned here, this is not meant to provide a one-size-fits-all program that could work at any museum. The best training program is unique to you and should be treated as a living program that needs to be carefully updated and edited as time goes on.

### TRAINING TOPICS

As you plan your training program, consider both onboarding training for new employees and ongoing training to help your team continue to improve at the same time. Begin by brainstorming a list of the topics you want to cover and fill in the details you want to share.

**Understanding Your Organization**

It's vital for both new and established employees to understand the overall organization and their roles. Frontline team members are important ambassadors for your institution, and you don't want them to feel like outsiders or as if their work exists in a silo separate from other departments.

As you share information about your museum, start from the beginning. Share the history of your museum along with any key individuals or dates. This also is a good time to answer some frequently asked questions. When was the building constructed? Was the building always a museum? Why is the institution named after a particular person or family? Who are those people and what did they do? Are they still involved in the museum or community? Has the museum been located elsewhere? What were the stages of the construction of the building or campus? Answering each of these questions will help your team understand your museum.

Staff members will also want to understand where their roles fit in the organization. How is the staff organized? Where do they fit in and who else is working with them? Who are some of the individuals they will interact with often? Who are the leaders of the organization? People feel more confident when they understand their roles and the roles of their colleagues. This is important in onboarding training, but there also is an opportunity to learn more about your colleagues over time. People enjoy learning about the jobs and projects of others. You could hold such training sessions for solely your frontline team, or you could use a format that allows various departments to present to the entire museum staff.

Your frontline team will be spending the majority of their time with visitors, so you need to share the visitor information you know with them. During onboarding training, you can present a version of the material you gathered in chapters 2 and 3 and build more detail from there. Start with some basic information like where the museum's visitors come from, who they visit with, and how long they stay. You also can dig deeper into visitors' previous experience level with museums and the feedback that you routinely hear. What is the museum usually praised for? What areas are you working to improve? You are constantly collecting new data, whether formally or informally, so you can continue to learn more about your visitors, and you should share that information with your team.

Your team also will need to be experts on the museum's campus. Be sure to offer new employees tours of each facility as well as information about how visitors move through the museum. Be sure employees are familiar with the map or visitor guide. You can design activities that let employees explore the museum on their own to increase their comfort level. If you have activities for visitors that move them through the museum, consider using those activities in your employee onboarding. The activities can help new employees get comfortable with the museum and the activity at the same time. Employees likely will help visitors with the activity in the future, and this gives them confidence as they have shared the same experience.

In many museums, the frontline team plays an important role in membership sales. Be sure team members understand not only the mechanics of selling a membership through the software system but also the thought processes of members. Why do people become members? Is their primary goal to support the mission of the museum or to receive benefits? Which benefits are important to them? How do these preferences vary among different groups? The motivation for families may be different from that of young professionals. Share any data that your development department has, and have your best salespeople share advice.

## Collections and Exhibitions

You want your frontline team to have a passion for the subject matter of your museum and to continue to grow their knowledge. Their existing passions for history, art, or science may have factored into their hiring, but you want to nurture their passions and help them gain more knowledge about your museum specifically. Museums are a topic about which learning is never complete. It's important to give new employees an introduction to your collections and exhibitions, but you will continue to build on that knowledge over time.

If you aren't sure where to start, there are a few approaches you can take. You could organize a simple training by asking your most experienced frontline team members to talk about their favorite objects or exhibitions to share with visitors. What do visitors find interesting? What questions do they have? These team members will likely present a variety of items that will give the entire team a great base of knowledge.

You also could focus on the top five favorite objects or installations in your museum. What is most popular with visitors? What do visitors ask about the most? Once you select the objects, provide resources on each one that give background information, the history of the item, details about the maker or creation process, and the key concepts or takeaways. Are there frequently asked questions employees should be prepared for? Include anything that helps your team become experts in the object or exhibition. Then employees can learn about five more objects or exhibitions at a time until they have learned about everything in the museum.

These training sessions are great opportunities to get others involved. You could include the director, curators, conservators, educators, and peers from the visitor services department. Each of these experts can either offer an overview tour of his or her area of expertise or focus on a few key objects. The more voices you can include, the better. This shows your team that their roles are important and worth the investment of others in the organization.

## Excellent Service

You selected people who enjoy serving visitors, but you should spend time talking about the exact type of service you expect. While part of providing good service comes naturally, it is a skill that includes both a natural ability and continued learning.

If you are in a group setting, you can start a great conversation by discussing general customer service. We all spend time as customers, so ask for examples of good and bad service. It's great if your team can share specific instances, but if the conversation doesn't naturally start flowing, share a few examples yourself. You can expand to include specific establishments that regularly provide great service or general characteristics that your team consider to be good or bad service. You also can ask them to define good customer service with a dictionary definition, a list of bullet points, a drawing, or anything else their imagination can produce. This could be done individually or in small groups and then shared with the larger group.

A key component of these discussions is how good and bad service can make you feel when you are the customer. These discussions get your team in the right frame of mind and focused on good service. As you move further into your team's training, you can refer back to these discussions. For example, if the group talks about the negative feelings they experience when they believe people aren't really listening to their situations, you can mention those feelings when you discuss listening skills and personalized service. Doing this reiterates that your team's instincts are correct and shows you are all on the same page.

### Starting with Warmth

Some people equate customer service with being nice. Niceties are important, but service goes deeper than that. You want to focus on all the ways your behavior can make people feel welcome.

When you talk about warm and genuine communication, focus on body language and tone of voice, in addition to the words and phrases that you choose. While studies vary on the exact percentage, a large portion of personal communication comes from body language and tone of voice. This leaves a significantly smaller portion based on the specific words you choose.

Your employees' body language should focus on being welcoming. The wrong body language could send unintended messages, such as they don't think someone belongs at the museum, they don't think someone will follow the rules, or someone is bothering them with questions. A simple and useful exercise is to discuss body language that could make an employee look frustrated, judgmental, intimidating, bored, or like they don't want to engage in conversation with visitors. In training, you can have all the participants stand up and demonstrate what they think such messages would look like. Watch what they do for each example and call out specific details. If an employee stands with arms crossed, one hip popped out, or hands on the hips, what message does that send? Once you discuss those postures and other examples, encourage your team to practice a neutral stance with their arms at their sides or behind them. Instruct them to focus on eye contact and to maintain neutral or positive facial expressions. You can lighten things up by having them demonstrate eye contact or facial expressions that don't work. You can also include photos or videos of your established team showing examples of good and bad body language.

When you discuss tone of voice, you want to allow the team to practice in the same way. Have a few people use the same words but with different tones of voice. You can choose a simple sentence such as "I'm happy to help" or even a single word such as "fine." Can frustration, annoyance, snobbery, or indifference be heard in anyone's voice? Can your team match the statement to the tone? Are there some tones that sound similar? Have team members ever had experiences in which someone said the right thing, but the tone of voice made them question it? Sincerity shows clearly in this area.

As you consider specific words or phrases you want your team to use or avoid, remember that long scripts do not sound genuine. Visitors want to feel like they have met unique people, not an impersonal army of clones. That said, you may have some rules you want staff to follow. Do you want them to answer questions with complete sentences? How should they offer assistance? Is there phrasing they should use with rule enforcement? They should avoid too much jargon and overly affectionate words such as "sweetie" or "honey" as those can alienate visitors.

*Learning about the Individual Visitor*

Your employees are not the only ones communicating through their body language, tone of voice, and word choice. Visitors are communicating in the same way. If your goal is to adjust service for each visitor, a key component is listening to the messages people are sending you.

Think about the emotions or messages you want your team to recognize in visitors. These could include frustration, boredom, intimidation, nervousness, or that they don't want to engage and would like to explore on their own. You can use similar exercises to the ones you used above. Ask people how they would recognize these emotions in others. What cues would someone give to convey these messages?

Nervous visitors may hunch up their shoulders or cross their arms in front of their bodies. Their nervousness might show also with small laughter, and some people are quick to explain their lack of expertise. If your employees notice these behaviors, what could they do to put the visitors at ease? Frustration shows with eye rolls, a raised voice, or loud exhales. If staff see visitors who are frustrated, they should maintain a normal volume themselves and try to find the source of the problem. Listening to someone, allowing the person to tell his or her whole story, and demonstrating empathy can go a long way. You also should discuss when employees should contact a manager. Procedures will vary by museum but should be clear to staff. In general, you want staff to err on the side of reaching out for assistance.

If visitors are trying to send a message that they aren't interested in conversation, they may turn away, avoid eye contact, take small steps backward, or give very limited responses to engagement attempts such as nods or "mmm-hmm" sounds. If staff aren't sure if visitors are interested in further engagement, they can start with very short facts or stories and look for these cues. If visitors respond with eye contact, keep their shoulders facing staff, and ask follow-up questions, they might like to engage more.

Listening is also an important way to learn about visitors. Listening exercises can get your employees refocused on the details of their interactions. You can combine listening and questioning skills with an exercise that is specific to your museum. Choose four items from your collection that are similar. These could be four paintings, trains, animals, or anything specific to the institution. Separate your employees into pairs and have each pair sit back to back. Give one person a picture of one of the objects. You could either have that person describe the object to their partner or allow the other partner to ask questions about the object. You could further limit conversations to only open or closed questions. Closed questions solicit a short response such as yes or no, a specific color, or a shape. Open questions prompt discussion: "What do you see? What do you think?" Once the partner who is guessing the object thinks they can picture it, give them a copy of the four choices to choose from so they can guess which of the four their partner described. Guessing may be harder than they think if you chose the four items wisely. Afterward, discuss which details were important in describing the objects. Which questions were particularly helpful? How are open or closed questions beneficial in the galleries? How could staff apply this to their work?

### Redefining "Above and Beyond"

The phrase "going above and beyond" is commonly used when talking about service. Talk to your team about what that idea means regarding the museum. Give some examples of tasks that are expected from them on a daily basis as well as examples of the opportunities to go truly beyond expectations.

For situations they will encounter often, you can tell them exactly what you want them to do. Situations might include printing driving directions for someone leaving the museum, offering to take a group photograph so everyone can be in the picture, running to the welcome desk to get children's activities rather than expecting visitors to navigate their way back to the desk on their own to get them, or looking up more information for visitors about an item on display. If these are standard expectations, and I would argue they should be, you need to be clear about that. Discussions like this also help staff understand your goals when they need to make decisions on their own.

### Freedom to Exceed Expectations

You can't be with your staff at all times. You will need to give guidelines to help your employees make good independent decisions. The Denver Museum of Nature and Science refers to this as providing guardrails wide enough to empower and narrow enough to guide. Allowing your staff members the independence to wow visitors will result in truly memorable experiences.

As you discuss special requests, use real examples staff may encounter. What should they do if someone asks for more chairs during a small gallery performance? In the museum store, what if someone asks to special-order an item in a different color? What if people ask for activities for children? As you discuss examples, what factors may change the response? These discussions not only tell staff what to do in specific situations but also help them in the future when new topics come up. Can they infer what you would like them to do?

**Figure 10.1.** *Source: Chrysler Museum of Art*

For unique situations, specific stories can help staff understand the type of service you want to provide and how much freedom they have. In one example, a few grandmothers were enjoying the museum separately with their grandchildren and were surprised to find someone dressed as a popular book character. Each wanted a photo of her grandchild with the character but did not have a camera. One employee took a photo with his own camera and printed the photo on regular printer paper. Another took a photo on her own device, offered to email the picture to the woman, and even helped the visitor understand how to check her email. This type of story shows that there often is more than one right answer. This wasn't a specific situation these staff members had been trained on, but they both understood that they should find a way to take the photos and get them to the visitor.

In other situations, you may have visitors who are frustrated by conditions that may or may not be the fault of the museum. Daily irritations such as weather, traffic, or a line for entry can start the visit off on the wrong foot. The Academy Museum of Motion Pictures gives its employees some freedom to surprise and delight visitors. Small gestures such as a complimentary coffee can make a big difference. Give staff concrete examples of what they are allowed to offer and support them in those efforts.

## Serving a Diverse Audience

Museums are resources for everyone, and as such, we have a responsibility to think about how we can best serve all of the diverse members of our communities. A commitment to equity means that we want to offer the same level of service to everyone, but that doesn't mean service needs to be identical. We should celebrate the differences among our visitors and adjust the experience to suit each of them.

### *Racial Equity*

People of color are currently underrepresented in the audiences of most of the museums in the United States. The American Alliance of Museums reports that minority populations represent 9 percent of current museum visitors compared to 34 percent of the population.[1] These numbers will vary by community and individual museum, but most museums will acknowledge that racial equity among museum visitors is an important area that needs improvement.

As we try to understand why these numbers are low, it's important to consider the history of museums. Some museums were segregated as recently as the 1960s. That will clearly be remembered by many communities. Even if individuals were not strictly prohibited from visiting, they may not have been truly welcomed. This is a tough past that we need to acknowledge and grow from. We need to earn the trust of our communities, and that takes time and effort. It also requires open conversations and listening to our communities.

For some individuals, museums were not a part of their lives as children, and they are still not active visitors. If an activity is not part of people's routines, it usually needs to be introduced to them through friends and family. If no one in these individuals' networks is a museumgoer, those people may be less likely to visit. You may have to work hard to introduce your museum and convince people they would enjoy the experience you have to offer.

It's also true that museum collections and exhibitions have not always reflected the accomplishments of non-white artists, scientists, and historymakers. If you want people to feel comfortable in your museum, they need to see themselves in your installations. Hopefully your curators are actively working to share these accomplishments through new collections and exhibitions. The frontline team needs to be prepared to talk about these additions. If visitors ask where the work of people of color can be seen in the museum, team members should have answers ready that show enthusiasm and familiarity with this work. Sharing a few options and their personal favorites helps show this enthusiasm. Stories of people of color are important to tell, and all staff members need to be ready to share them.

Look closely at the feedback you have received from people of color to see how you can improve. You may find that those people are more likely to feel followed or singled out. It's an unfortunate reality that these individuals may have experienced unfair treatment at other businesses, and you want to make sure it doesn't occur at your museum. Talk openly with your team about how to prevent this from happening. Using examples can help facilitate this challenging discussion. If your employees' jobs require them to make regular rounds through public spaces, they will have moments when they will pass the same visitors several times. Brainstorm with your team how they could lighten those situations so no one feels followed. One employee may chat with the visitor and explain his or her role, and another may make a joke about walking in circles. The important takeaway is that ignoring the awkwardness will not make visitors feel less followed; it will make the situation worse.

In another example, you may have a rule that requires an employee to check inside all bags over a certain size at the main entrance. A group of women enter at the same time and they all have bags. There is only one woman of color in the group, and she has the only large bag. Singling her out has the potential to be perceived very poorly. If you check her bag only, you should be sure to share the rule about size. A preferable option is to simply check all the bags in the group. With this method, no one feels singled out and the group likely doesn't even give the search a second thought.

Employees may have their own implicit biases toward people who are not like them, and it is beneficial to everyone to look inside themselves, recognize their biases, and actively work to overcome them. There are training programs available for the workplace that you can implement to help employees grow, which will result in a better experience for visitors. If you hear feedback from visitors that they were treated differently due to their ethnicity, you need to try to understand what led to this perception, apologize to the visitor, and work with both the individual employee and the team to prevent the same thing from reoccurring.

Your human resources department has likely shared procedures for reporting racism from employees. You also will need to discuss what employees should do if they observe racism from visitors, directed at either employees or fellow visitors. As discussed in chapter 8, this cannot be tolerated in any way, and you need to be sure that is very clear to your team. Strict policies like this help create more inclusive museums.

*Accessibility*

As your staff consider how to welcome all your visitors, they must include the 26 percent of the population that has some type of disability.[2] It's important that we consider how to make our museums welcoming and accessible to these individuals.

While there are some tips and recommendations below, it is always preferable to hear directly from individuals with disabilities themselves. There are a lot of videos available that show some of the difficulties these individuals face in their daily lives. Watching people participate in familiar activities, such as shopping or traveling, can help your team relate to these individuals and can motivate them to provide a welcoming atmosphere. This also is a great opportunity to work with community partners. These partners can provide staff training and give feedback about the museum experience from their perspectives.

For visitors who are blind or have low vision, you can begin by making sure that your employees know how to guide someone with their arm. The visitor lightly holds the employee's arm just above the elbow and follows their movements. There are many videos that show how to properly do this. Be sure to stress that this should be offered, not insisted on. Staff should not touch any visitors without their permission, but this is particularly true for visitors who are blind or have low vision and may not see staff members as they approach. Staff members also should be familiar with white canes. These help someone understand their surroundings through various techniques, including dragging the cane back and forth to find obstacles and tapping the ground to hear the echo off nearby buildings. The white cane also is used as a signal to others so they may be aware of the person's disability. Employees should understand and offer the resources the museum may have available to assist visitors with low vision, such as magnifying glasses available to visitors in the galleries or visitor guides available in large print.

Your museum may offer touch tours that can be scheduled through your education department. These tours allow visitors to touch approved objects in your collection while wearing gloves. This is usually accompanied by thorough visual description. If this is something you do offer, see if your frontline team could receive some training. You may not be able to offer a full tour on the spot, but an experience with one or two objects could make a large impact on that visitor.

As you think about how to welcome visitors who are deaf or hard of hearing, think about any experiences in your museum that are focused on sound. How can you help visitors enjoy those activities? If you offer an audio tour, is there a written transcript available? If there are videos in your spaces, are there captions? If not, could you create written transcripts? Many people can read lips, so if visitors are struggling to understand you, try facing them and speaking clearly. If that doesn't help, try writing things down. For visitors who wear hearing aids, there are induction loops available, both mobile and installed in a specific space like an auditorium, that allow projected sound to feed directly into hearing aids. Be sure your team knows where this system may be available and how it works.

Museums can be difficult to navigate for people in wheelchairs or who use walkers or canes. If you offer loaner wheelchairs to visitors, your team members can take turns exploring the museum while seated in wheelchairs. After this experience, they will not know what it is like to have a disability, but they will have a better idea of the difficulties people may experience during museum visits. Are there tight corners? Are displays at a height that makes them easy to enjoy from a lower vantage point? Is signage easy to see? Are ramps and elevators easy to find? What is the experience like at the admission desk? Are there small changes that could make the visit easier? For example, if the counters at the welcome desk or in the museum store are tall, consider placing a small clipboard at each location to make it easier for visitors in wheelchairs to sign their receipts. Be sure your team understands that they can offer assistance to people in wheelchairs or offer loaner wheelchairs to people using walkers or canes, but they should not make assumptions or insist.

Visitors with cognitive, developmental, or emotional disabilities will each experience the museum differently and you want to be as flexible as possible. Some individuals will be anxious about visiting a museum if they don't know what to expect. Look at your museum's website and see if you can share information in a social story to show what visitors experience on the campus. Museums also can be overwhelming for individuals with sensory issues. Consider days and times when you reduce the amount of lighting and noise in certain spaces to allow for more comfortable visits for these individuals. You also can designate spaces where visitors can take a break away from public areas. Be open to feedback from visitors and be flexible whenever possible. For example, if a group has a chaperone who feels he needs to hold the hands of two participants, perhaps consider making an exception to your backpack rule and allow him to wear his bag regularly on his back. If your programs are designed for specific ages, are there ways older children or adults could participate if they wanted to? Empower your frontline team to react in the moment and help each individual have a great experience.

The Americans with Disabilities Act requires you to allow service animals in your museum, and you should want to welcome them as well. These animals allow visitors with disabilities to visit your museum. Only dogs or miniature horses legally qualify as service animals, and the only questions you can ask are "Is this a service animal?" and "What work or task has the animal been trained to perform?" You are not required to admit other types of animals or comfort or therapy animals, but you should consider allowing them whenever possible. These animals play important roles in the lives of visitors, and visitors may not feel comfortable visiting without them. Your goal is to help as many people as possible enjoy your museum, and these animals may be the difference between someone participating or staying home.

Be sure your employees understand the laws and your museum's policies. You also should discuss the wide array of services that these animals are trained to provide. Some people are aware of guide dogs for only individuals who are blind, but these animals can be trained for many tasks. Understanding these tasks can help your team understand visitors' needs. Watching videos of individuals with service animals can be a helpful way to share this information.

It is required that service animals be under the control of their handlers. If an animal is not under control or not housebroken, you can ask that the animal be removed but be clear that the visitor is welcome without the companion. You likely want this sensitive and rare situation to be handled by a manager. Your employees should know when to call for help in these situations.

### LGBTQIA+ Visitors

Members of the LGBTQIA+ community may not feel welcome in all public spaces, and you want to make sure that they do feel welcome in your museum. This portion of training should be about awareness and familiarity with terminology and should offer helpful tips.

Terms like "gender identity," "sexual orientation," and "gender expression" may be new to some of your employees. There are several ways to share these definitions with your team. There are online videos and print resources that do a good job defining these terms. This language is evolving, so be sure to use up-to-date resources. These resources may also discuss which questions are acceptable to ask and which are not. For example, you can ask people's preferred pronouns or names, and then it is important to use those moving forward. Personal questions about people's transitions are not acceptable.

Working with a community partner can be helpful when discussing this topic. The Chrysler Museum of Art partnered with Equality Virginia to provide a training session for staff and volunteers. This included an understanding of some of the difficulties the LGBTQIA+ community faces, some important terminology, and some helpful hints for providing service. The museum continues to provide an abbreviated version of this training as part of its onboarding program.

If your team members are responsible for dividing individuals into groups for any reason, avoid dividing by gender as that can alienate some participants. If you are guiding activities for families, remember that families come in many different forms, and assumptions can be alienating. This includes not only the LGBTQIA+ community but also single parents, grandparents, and older siblings. A small change in language can make a big difference. For example, if children are working on a craft project and there is a step during which they will need help, consider saying "Ask your adult to help you with this step" instead of "Ask your mom to help you with this step."

In your training, you also will need to discuss restrooms. You should make it clear that individuals can use the restrooms they prefer. While visitors can make the choices best for them, your team should be familiar with where single-occupancy restrooms are located as they are preferred by many people, including families, caregivers assisting others with restrooms, and members of the LGBTQIA+ community. If someone asks for directions to the restroom and you aren't sure which restroom the person would prefer, offer all options. "The men's room is on the left, the women's room is on the right, and there is a single-occupancy restroom straight ahead."

## Language Barriers

All museums should talk about language barriers and how to greet visitors whose primary language is not English (or the common language where the museum is located). The exact topics will vary by museum based on the community and visitors. If there is another language that is prominent in your community, it should also be prominent in your museum. This could include using that language on wall labels, on wayfinding signage, and in programs and hiring bilingual staff members.

For a wider range of languages, you can produce multiple versions of your visitor guide or map. You can also focus on key phrases in multiple languages. These could be taught in a training session and made available in a written resource at the admission desk or at other important locations. These phrases could include welcoming language, pricing, rule enforcement, and emergency communications.

You likely have colleagues throughout your institution who speak a variety of languages. Consider making a list with this information to share with the frontline team. If staff are having trouble communicating with visitors, who can they call for help? Employees also can try to write things down as visitors' reading skills in foreign languages may be better than their speaking skills. Employees can use existing technology to help them communicate, but they shouldn't rely solely on those programs as they work better for some languages than for others.

## Visitor Types or Personas

You may have defined different visitor types or personas specific to your institution. You may have chosen to incorporate types from national data or to create your own based on what you know about your museum's visitors. Whichever you chose, you can make visitor personas be a key part of your training.

For each of your visitor types, your training should include background information, how to recognize visitors who may match with each type, and what style of service each visitor type may or may not enjoy. For example, at the Chrysler Museum of Art, an "art information sponge" is familiar with art terminology, is comfortable in museums, and loves to learn more about works of art. This type enjoys learning in a variety of ways, including audio tours, wall labels, formal tours, interactive activities, and interactions with staff. You can identify this type by listening to the language people use when talking about art and by observing how much they interact with interpretation options, such as wall labels and audio tours. Visitors of this type would welcome conversation about art and want to know about the engagement options available to them.

After providing information about your visitor types in a presentation and/or handout, you can reinforce the types with an exercise in which you discuss example visitors. This gives you the chance to move past general descriptions to what staff may really see on the job. For example, you might start with an art information sponge by describing a visitor who asks at the welcome desk about the museum's impressionist paintings. You later observe the visitor listening to the audio tour while reading labels and waiting for the docent tour to start. Ask your staff what type of visitor they believe this is, reinforce their knowledge by asking what they can infer about the visitor, and ask staff to put this information into practice by determining what they would do next if they encountered that visitor. This exercise could be done individually on a worksheet or in a small-group discussion.

The final step is to send staff to the galleries to observe real visitors. You will, of course, need to talk about discretion. You do not want visitors to feel like they are being followed through the museum. Ask staff to observe a few visitors, perhaps at specific locations, such as observing one group during their initial conversation at the admission desk and another in the galleries. Ask staff to note what types of visitors these may be, what that might tell staff about the visitors, and what staff may say while interacting with those visitors. When you come back together as a group, allow everyone to talk about the visitors they observed, what conclusions they drew, and what ideas they had. You also should ask them to include descriptions of the visitors. This allows you to see if different people observed the same individuals or groups at different moments. Did staff members infer different things about those visitors, or did they make the same observations?

As you wrap up your discussion on visitor types, remind your team that everyone visiting the museum is a unique individual. These personas are meant to help staff understand visitors, not to put visitors in boxes. This is why watching visitors' body language and communication is so important.

**Safety and Security**

You will need to cover security procedures in your training, but the specifics will vary greatly by job type. Chapter 8 discusses blending security and service, but no matter how your team is structured, museum security is part of everyone's responsibility, and there are some things everyone working with the public should know.

You want to be very clear about the rules that each employee will need to enforce. These could include policies about ticketing, bag checks, photography, capacity, and more. Be sure employees understand the reasoning behind each rule so they are comfortable discussing them with visitors. Be clear about how you want staff to enforce these rules. You likely want them to start with a friendly tone, avoid embarrassing visitors, and follow up with the reasoning behind the rules. Some employees may struggle enforcing rules, so training sessions are good opportunities for role-playing or other repetition.

You should discuss visitor behavior that could be a security concern, including people being too interested in museum operations. Some people are simply curious, but others may be trying to gain information that could be used to commit crimes. The specifics will vary by museum, but suspicious visitor behavior may include asking specific questions about staff coverage or rotations, security features like cameras or door access, the values of objects, or where items are stored. You also may observe visitors not following normal traffic patterns, such as moving unusually quickly or slowly or taking photographs of security features and staff rather than their friends and the exhibitions.

Tell your staff what to do if they observe unusual behavior. Who do they report it to? As mentioned previously, you need to make sure they don't jump to conclusions and still provide those visitors with great service. Some people are simply interested in how museums run or behave a little differently, and that is certainly allowed. Remind your team that interacting with visitors is in itself a security measure. Greeting visitors alerts them that the facility is well staffed while it also provides a warm welcome.

### Emergency Procedures

Everyone in the museum has a role in an emergency, especially frontline staff. You want to be sure your team is ready to handle any emergency, including evacuating the museum for a fire alarm, an injured visitor, a missing child, an active shooter, or a natural disaster such as a tornado or earthquake. The procedures for each of these situations should be clearly written and readily available.

Emergency preparedness is an area where details and repetition are important. You want your employees to feel confident that they know how to handle each of these situations. They need to understand both their roles and the roles of others. During onboarding training, you should provide information on the procedures for these situations and make sure employees know who will take the lead during these times. Be sure to walk around and physically show them exits and meeting places. Remember that staff are still learning your campus and museums can be very complex places.

Moving forward, see how you can incorporate safety into the museum's normal operations. Perhaps you could include safety tips in your regular staff meetings or post first-aid information in staff areas. Keep the information fresh in employees' minds. Periodic drills are necessary, and they are most effective when you include as many departments as possible. After each drill or actual emergency, take the time to debrief with your team. What went right or wrong? What would have been different if X occurred instead of Y? Some of these scenarios are discussed in chapter 8, and discussions about emergencies can help everyone be more prepared in the future.

### General Information

As you wrap up your list of training topics, be sure to include basic information that you will need to cover. Allot time for onboarding paperwork and orientation from human resources. Cover topics specific to the job, such as dress code, how to request time off, how to clock in and out, and some of the specifics of employees' daily assignments. Plan for training on software procedures, job-specific equipment, and tour techniques.

## TRAINING STYLES AND TOOLS

You now have a list of the information you would like to cover, both in your initial onboarding training and in subsequent continuing instruction. Now it's time to consider *how* you will share the information.

You have several options, and you need to choose the right tool for the right job. There may be some topics that you choose to cover in multiple ways in order to reinforce your key ideas.

Managers at the Academy Museum of Motion Pictures consider different learning styles as they plan their training, and therefore they present information in a variety of ways. They know their employees will benefit in different ways from reading about a topic, watching videos, and watching someone else perform a task. In addition to different formats, they also try to consider potential accommodations, such as captions or large print. They want to plan for and include the accommodations before employees have to ask for them. This repetition, variety, and customization allows them to make sure each individual employee benefits equitably from the training.

### Gallery Tours

One of the most common training methods is to offer tours of your galleries to new and existing employees. New employees will need a broad introduction to the collections. This may be a brief introduction to all areas, including an explanation of the flow between areas. Why are things arranged in this way? What is the story you are trying to tell visitors?

There is always more to learn, so you can add depth to different topics over time. As mentioned earlier, tours are great opportunities to include colleagues from other departments. Curators, educators, and other colleagues can share their expertise. You can record these tours and build your library over time. You can add more detail on popular exhibitions, highlight new acquisitions, answer visitor questions, or simply allow scholars to share their new research.

You also should coach your team to ask questions and truly engage with the colleagues leading the tours. Such interactions build the relationships between individuals and make the process more enjoyable for those leading the tours.

### Classroom Training

Traditional classroom training allows you to move through presentations, encourage discussion, and reinforce new concepts with hands-on exercises. For onboarding training, this model works well when you have several employees starting at the same time. They can quickly form

**Figure 10.2.** *Source: Chrysler Museum of Art*

a camaraderie with one another, which prevents them from feeling alone as the newbies. The classroom model may not work as well if you need to hire on a near-constant rolling basis, but it can be used for ongoing training as you bring employees together to focus on specific topics.

Try to make the training environment comfortable. When possible, allow employees to dress as they like for training. As you set up the classroom, think again about comfort. Choose a comfortable room and chairs if you have options. Arrange the room in a way that will allow for small-group work. It's great if you are able to provide food and drink; even offering water and a few sweet treats can make a difference in helping people feel welcome and ready to focus. You can complete the room by providing paper to take notes or draw and small items to play with, as that helps some people concentrate.

A slide presentation will likely be a key component of classroom training and is a good way to organize and convey your thoughts. Be sure your slides are easy to read from every seat in the room. Don't list your ideas word for word on your slides, but rather highlight key points. Use images to break things up and be sure one slide isn't on display for too long. If you have a lot of detailed information in your presentation, be sure to provide the material in print, whether as a copy of the presentation or in another format.

Large-group discussions get people involved and add depth to topics by using real examples. You likely will discover that there are some individuals who are more comfortable speaking up than others. You need those talkers to make your training successful, but you also need to allow others to speak. Remember that not everyone is comfortable speaking in front of a large group, particularly if they are starting new roles. Breaking into small groups allows every individual to speak and contribute. Small groups also help employees form relationships with new colleagues. A balance of large- and small-group discussions throughout the training session is ideal.

Role-playing can be beneficial, particularly with rule enforcement, answering frequently asked questions, or dealing with frustrated visitors. Since standing in front of a large group can be very intimidating to some people, consider either asking volunteers to demonstrate in front of a large group or working on these situations in pairs or small groups.

As you plan the schedule for the training, you want to avoid having everyone sit still for too long. You want people to be attentive and alert. Your presentation will provide the outline for the session, but be sure to break up the session with videos, discussions, and exercises. Leave yourself some flexibility to change things up based on how the session goes. Each time you lead this training, it will be different. Some groups may need more breaks, some may have more active group discussions, and others may spend more time on specific topics. Build room for this flexibility into your schedule.

## Self-Guided Training

Independent learning is well suited for situations in which people may be starting with different levels of experience. This type of learning allows them to learn at their own paces. Topics for which this might be useful include technical instructions, deeper content on subject matter, or any training that encourages employees to look inside themselves. This also is useful if you need to provide training to people at different times. If you can't gather everyone together, independent learning ensures you are providing everyone with the same information.

### Putting It in Writing

Written resources are relatively inexpensive and easy to produce. Technical manuals with step-by-step instructions and screenshots are great for new staff members as they learn standard procedures and gain confidence in everyday skills. Written resources also are useful for items that don't come up often. For example, if gift memberships are most popular in December, even your most seasoned employees may forget the process and rely on a handy guide for reassurance in July.

Printed materials also can be used for content resources that are built over time. For example, you can create a brief document about an object or exhibition in your museum. It may include relevant definitions, biographies, frequently asked questions, material, processes, and other key information. Once you create a sample and format, you can add more, similar entries. These entries can be created by multiple people on your team, so individuals can write about the subjects they are most interested in and about which they have expertise. You can create written materials about many topics, including the vendors in the museum store, the plants in the garden, or other industry-specific information.

### Using Technology

If you'd like to take a more modern approach, consider a learning-management system. Your museum's human resources department may already utilize such a system to cover key topics such as harassment, workplace safety, and management skills. If that department doesn't have such a system, you may be able to partner with them on the purchase if you can show how the system could be used across the museum. Learning-management systems allow information to be delivered in individual courses that people can watch at their own paces. Courses could include informational slides, videos, or interviews with experts. If a course covers a topic new to employees or is particularly challenging, employees may want to watch a segment multiple times. Allowing courses to be completed independently helps level the playing field for employees who may have very different levels of experience with topics or learn at different paces.

The Broad and the Academy Museum of Motion Pictures both use learning-management systems to cover a wide variety of topics, including customer service, rule enforcement, and each object on display. Each module ends with an assessment to be sure that the major concepts are understood. These courses are devised for specific departments, but they are available to all employees. For example, visitor service associates could watch courses about proper art-handling techniques or conservation, which could help them as they consider the next steps in their careers. There are some courses that apply to multiple departments, such as how to write an incident report, and courses that cover topics very specific to the museum, such as how film stock works at the Academy Museum.

There are endless possibilities for learning-management systems as new content can continue to be created and new employees can watch new and old courses.

### Shadowing

It's great to learn about the job you will be doing through reading and lectures, but there is nothing like watching someone in action. Shadowing is an important step in the training process and involves pairing a seasoned employee with a new employee. The seasoned employee goes about his or her job as normal, modeling excellent behavior and explaining processes.

Since all your employees likely handle tasks a little differently, it's useful to allow new employees to shadow a mix of team members. If new employees observe a few different ways to approach situations, they can find their own style and voice.

You will need to spend time preparing your staff to be shadowed. You may think that it will be easy for them to just go about their jobs and the new employees will soak up the excellent behavior. That might happen, but it might not, and you will be much more successful if you tell seasoned employees more about what you want them to do. You should stress the main concepts you want them to convey as well as specific tasks such as opening and closing procedures, standard transactions, frequently asked questions, and where supplies are stored. They need to be reminded to demonstrate great behavior and not get distracted chatting with their new coworkers to the point that they ignore visitors. You also should tell them some simple teaching steps for standard processes such as sales transactions. They should demonstrate those processes a few times, then let new employees try transactions while they observe and coach. Spend a little time observing this process to see if any seasoned employees need a little more coaching in providing good feedback.

Shadowing is an important step in the training process, but it shouldn't be the only step. The danger of moving straight to shadowing without any prior discussion is that you lose the overarching concepts and the big ideas. Shadowing is great for specific tasks, but why are you doing things this way? What are your goals with service? You want to strike the right balance between conceptual ideas and practical instruction.

## DRAFTING YOUR PLAN

Now you have a list of topics you want to cover and a list of the delivery techniques available to you. It's time to make a plan.

First, look at all your topics. Note how each topic will be covered in onboarding training and which will be covered at another time. Many topics may fit into both categories. For some, you may give basic information initially and then build upon that knowledge. For others, you may present all the information up front but plan to repeat it from time to time so it stays fresh. Each role in your museum is a little different. You may have people who are hired to do very narrow lists of tasks and others whose jobs are very complex. While you may cover a similar list of topics with both sets of employees, the depth may vary, so customize the program for each role.

Once you have your topics listed, start lining them up with the delivery methods you think will most effectively communicate the information. How long would you like to spend on each topic? Who should be trained on it? There likely will be one or two department leaders who lead most of the training, but look for ways to include others. For onboarding training, could the director come and greet the group on the first day? Could each curator give a brief tour of their area? Could someone from development come talk about membership? How can you include your frontline team? These same principles apply to ongoing training. How can you showcase the expertise of your colleagues?

Unfortunately, you may not be able to include all the training you'd like right away. You may map out everything you would like to do and discover that your ideal onboarding training includes ten full classroom days followed by two days of self-study and three days of shadowing. Odds are, you will not have the budget for that much training, and you will need to revise your plan. What can you afford? How can you advocate for your vision in the next budget cycle?

Once you have your plan, you will need to prepare your team. For onboarding, map out the full training process and prepare the team for what to expect. Tell them what to wear and if they need to bring anything. Be sure to be specific about meals. Will meals be provided? If employees bring their own meals, is there a refrigerator or microwave available? Is there an area to purchase food and drinks? For later training, share topics ahead of time to allow as many team members as possible to participate. No matter how you are presenting the information, consider recording it in some way so you can share it in the future.

## TESTING EMPLOYEES' KNOWLEDGE

As you plan your training, particularly onboarding training, be sure to allow time at the end for reviewing and testing. Testing could be worksheets, computer quizzes, role playing, or a combination of all these techniques. These exercises provide a chance to clarify anything that was not covered or was confusing. For onboarding training, this also gives new employees confidence that they have the information they need to succeed in their new roles.

These training resources do not need to live in only one department. You should encourage all departments to share training and expertise with one another. Sharing knowledge extends ideas and values throughout the institution, establishes a shared culture among the entire museum team, and shows the frontline team that they are a valued part of the organization.

## NOTES

1. *Demographic Transformation and the Future of Museums*, Center for the Future of Museums
2. "Disability Impacts All of Us," Centers for Disease Control and Prevention, https://www.cdc.gov /ncbddd/disabilityandhealth/documents/disabilities_impacts_all_of_us.pdf

# 11

## Building Strong Morale and a Professional Frontline Team

You've spent some time establishing the structure of your frontline team; now it's time to ensure your employees feel like a vital part of the greater museum team. Unfortunately, these employees do not always feel they are treated as museum professionals within their own institutions. At times, they are treated like a separate group, disconnected from the staff who work behind the scenes. You want to be sure that you offer the same benefits, opportunities, and resources to the frontline team as you offer to their colleagues. Small details can have a large impact on how staff feel about their workplace.

### R-E-S-P-E-C-T, FIND OUT WHAT IT MEANS TO THEM

Everyone wants to be respected at work and the frontline team is no different. There are some tips below to help your team feel this respect, but the most important thing is to listen and find out what makes a difference to them. A strong manager will be open to feedback and make continuous changes to be sure the team feels supported and understood.

#### Respecting Their Humanity

Some frontline managers feel that the best way to manage their teams is to strictly control every aspect of their employees' behavior with demoralizing and unnecessary rules. This often is a sign of an inexperienced and ineffectual manager. The simple understanding that your employees are individuals who will need flexibility and understanding will have a huge impact on morale and will improve overall performance. You want to avoid making broad, controlling policies for the group because one person behaved inappropriately.

The worst of these rules monitors the restroom habits of staff. We all remember the feeling of panic from childhood when a teacher would not let you use the restroom. This is something that should not exist in the workplace. Staff members need to understand that they can use the restroom whenever they need. They may be required to get coverage before they can leave their posts, but this should be a simple and clear process. They should not be made to feel as if they are a burden because of these breaks. Some people may need to use the restroom more frequently, and that should be respected. True abuse of these policies is rare and can be addressed directly.

You also should carefully consider your policies on dress code, cell-phone use, and similar topics. Dress-code policies should be intended to make your staff easily identifiable and to present a professional image. It is not necessary to create clones. Be flexible where you can and allow your employees to showcase a bit of their personalities while still maintaining the museum's standards. If you have existing policies that restrict hair color, tattoos, or piercings, you should take time to consider if they are still necessary. Styles evolve, and if the policies are not necessary for your museum, you may miss out on talented people.

Clearly, you don't want your team members to be on their phones all day, but reconsider strict policies that do not allow them to carry phones at all. Staff members may use their phones to check the time or to look things up for visitors. They may also simply want to be reachable in case of emergency. If specific employees can't responsibly carry their phones, then you can require those individuals to leave their phones in their lockers. However, it's not necessary to make this policy universal.

Naturally, employees will be sick from time to time, and sick employees should stay home. You want to be clear about the procedures for calling in sick, including the length of notice and the preferred communication method. There should be absolutely no guilt involved in this process. Yes, these situations are challenging for managers, but that is the manager's responsibility, and it should not be passed on to employees. If employees call or text to say they are sick, the only reply should be that you hope they feel better soon. Museums certainly can and should set attendance policies, but those policies are clearly communicated ahead of time and are enforced equally with all team members. The policies are in place to prevent excessive tardiness and absenteeism; they do not require sick employees to come to work.

### Respecting Their Breaks

You want your staff to be at their best when they are "on stage." In public spaces, you expect them to be friendly and helpful and to let negative interactions roll off their backs as much as possible. This is much easier to achieve if you allow them moments when they can genuinely be "off stage." The opportunity to recharge is valuable and results in better vigilance and service.

In addition to allowing the ad hoc bathroom breaks mentioned above, build a structure that allows your staff to take much-needed breaks. You should include a short break on all shifts and sufficient meal breaks on longer shifts. Everyone needs a moment to text home about dinner, have a snack, or simply get off their feet for a moment. It's easy for someone whose job is primarily in an office, who can do these things with relative ease, to forget what it's like to have limited access to these simple necessities.

On occasion, staff members' breaks may be delayed by visitor interactions. You clearly want staff to help each visitor, so you need to assure them that they will be able to take their full breaks, even if they start their breaks late. They need to be confident that this is automatic and not at all an imposition on their supervisors or coworkers. If guaranteed and protected breaks are part of your team culture, your team will feel more appreciated.

### Respecting Their Individuality

Each staff member is an individual and wants to be treated as such. Staff want to be recognized for their strengths, have their preferences considered, and feel like unique members of the team.

We all have roles in our lives beyond being employees. Team members are also spouses, parents, friends, students, artists, animal lovers, and more. They will appreciate the recognition of these other roles and the impact those roles may have on their work. Sometimes the impact is ongoing, such as parents or caregivers needing to be reachable in case of emergency. Others have short-term needs, such as when they are buying a new home. We all know this can be a complicated process. During that time, they may need to take extra phone calls or afternoons off to complete the closings. Your flexibility during these times shows a level of understanding that will be appreciated by staff.

Each team member will have unique interests, knowledge, and strengths. Look for opportunities for them to grow and share these talents in their roles. There may be extra projects that are well suited to specific individuals, both within their own departments and in other departments. Someone who is good with technology and is organized may be responsible for recording and organizing staff training sessions. Someone who hopes for a future career in museum education may create an activity for a family program to help the education department. If someone is an expert in a particular topic related to your museum, allow that person to lead a training session and share his or her expertise with colleagues.

### Scheduling Details

All managers consider their staff members' formal schedule requests, but great managers also consider individual preferences. Perhaps you know that someone is willing to work Saturdays when needed but, if possible, prefers to work other days so they can attend their child's baseball games. Another employee may like to sleep in and will prefer shifts with a later start time when possible. One person may share that they have trouble staying on their feet all day and prefer shorter shifts, while someone with a longer commute may prefer to work longer shifts fewer times per week. These are the types of requests that cannot always be honored, but when you can honor them as often as possible, you help your staff members feel appreciated and respected as individuals. Staff will also be more likely to be flexible and will help you with the schedule when they can.

### Recognizing and Acknowledging Their Achievements

Everyone likes to be recognized and appreciated for the work they do. In addition to informally providing feedback on a consistent basis, be sure you put systems in place for various types of recognition.

Performance appraisals are an important feedback opportunity for all employees. They are a time to reflect on the successes of the past year, address any concerns, and set goals for the coming year. Some people may think that frontline staff aren't interested in this kind of formal appraisal, but you'll find that many appreciate the time with their managers and the feedback. They want to know that their strengths are recognized and learn how they can improve. They also may like this time to discuss their future goals with their managers.

Your museum may have recognition systems available to all staff members. These may be displays in public areas or announcements at all-staff meetings. Be sure to include your frontline teams with this type of recognition. You may provide recognition for years of service or for outstanding performances. At a departmental level, dedicate a few minutes at each department meeting to celebrate your team's successes. This gives the frontline team the opportunity to recognize the times that coworkers have offered great service or helped colleagues. You also could simply acknowledge that the team worked well together on a busy day. Celebrating your team's successes adds a positive tone to your staff meetings and allows for consistent opportunities for recognition.

There may be opportunities for recognition in your local community or within your museum networks. Some local tourism bureaus or similar entities offer awards for frontline employees at various times of year. If these awards exist, you should participate and allow your staff members to help select nominees. There may also be awards or recognition opportunities available through museum associations. Recognition from beyond your institution is a special honor for your outstanding team members.

## LISTENING TO AND INCLUDING THEM

Your frontline team members have a lot of expertise, both in the knowledge they arrived with and what they gained while working at your museum. They are experts on your visitors, and their experience is valuable to others in the museum.

### Carefully Choosing Language

When it comes to making someone feel included as a vital part of the museum team, small things can make a big difference. The language you use can be very powerful.

Sometimes museums are looking for ways to describe their administrative or office staff. This group includes those who work Monday through Friday in departments such as curatorial, registration, and finance and excludes those on the front line such as security and visitor services. This distinction should be made rarely and only when needed. An example of when this distinction may be important is when a holiday falls on a Sunday and you want to clarify that it will be observed on Monday for those who work Monday through Friday and will vary for others based on their schedules. It is not necessary or prudent to separate staff based on perceived importance or professionalism. Every department and team member plays an important role and should be treated as such. If you do determine that it's necessary to make this type of distinction, choose your words carefully. Referring to only a portion of the staff as regular staff or professional staff is hurtful and should be avoided. Everyone is a professional at what they do.

On a similar note, avoid sweeping statements that don't apply to everyone. For example, don't make a large production of wishing everyone an enjoyable long holiday weekend if it isn't a long weekend for everyone. In addition to not excluding those who do not have the time off, find a way to thank those who do need to work on holidays. A public thank-you and food on the holiday can go a long way.

Meetings in which all staff members come together can be very beneficial. These meetings are good opportunities for face-to-face time with colleagues from other departments and for everyone to share the museum's accomplishments and upcoming events. These meetings should be scheduled at a time when all departments can attend, which likely means before the museum opens for the day. Adjust the schedules of frontline staff so they have time to attend and still complete their opening duties. If everyone can't attend, it is not truly an all-staff meeting. If you have cross-departmental meetings that do not include these frontline departments, you need to find different names for the meetings. Ideally, you would find ways to include the frontline team and their expertise.

## Gatherings

In addition to all-staff meetings, casual gatherings are great times for employees to build relationships with their coworkers. These relationships include those with colleagues in their own departments, people in other departments whose work intersects with theirs, and staff who they might not see often. Casual activities might include lunches, happy hours, chili cookoffs, pie-baking contests, or other social activities.

As you plan these events, be aware of the varied schedules of your staff. If you are planning a breakfast, consider the start times of various teams as well as the opening time of the museum. For lunches, you will likely need to plan for a larger window of time, rather than one specific meeting time, to accommodate everyone who needs to retain coverage for admissions, security, and the museum store; these people will need to rotate and take turns attending the event. If leaders are available, they should help cover those team members' positions so everyone has a chance to attend. For evening activities, consider the clock-out times of all teams as well as the closing time of the museum.

If the activity is for all staff members, you want to be sure everyone can attend. This can be a challenge with competing schedules, so if you aren't able to find one solution that works for everyone, be sure to vary the activities over time. This may mean varying the type of activity, day of the week, and time of day. Your facilities team may leave work at 3 o'clock while the museum doesn't close until 5 o'clock. Facilities workers may not want to wait around for an event to start. They may rather participate in a breakfast or lunch. Adding variety helps everyone feel considered and appreciated.

A common benefit for employees is a complimentary museum membership. Events for members are enjoyable and it's common to find groups of employees from various departments socializing at these events. These events require a lot of assistance from frontline staff to run smoothly. If these team members want to attend as guests, you should try to honor as many requests as possible and rotate who is able to attend while others work.

## Listening to Their Ideas

Your team members are the ones interacting directly with visitors, so you should take the time to listen to their feedback. You should ask them what they are hearing from visitors. How are visitors responding to a new exhibition? What questions do they have about a specific object? Are they watching the new video?

Give staff multiple avenues to provide this feedback, including honest discussions at meetings, an open door to discuss these items with their managers, and a way to submit visitor feedback in writing. If each team member takes a moment to write down one piece of feedback each day, you will gather a lot of responses and increase your understanding of your museum's visitors. Feedback may include a compliment directed toward a specific staff member, a great quote about an exhibition, or a point of confusion or frustration from someone's visit. These comments can be useful to observe patterns and see areas of strength and opportunities for improvement. They can be useful also when the museum is looking for quotes from visitors about specific topics. Assign one team member to gather and organize this feedback.

In addition to communicating visitor feedback, the team may have ideas for improvement. Perhaps they believe an object is being touched frequently and a physical barrier would help. They may propose a new sign that would help visitors navigate the museum. Listen to their ideas and give each one careful consideration. Not all ideas will be implemented, but employees should not feel discouraged from presenting other ideas in the future. If something is not possible, explain the reasoning as this will help staff grow and deepen their understanding of the museum.

Include representatives from the front line in cross-departmental teams. Their participation is useful for the museum and rewarding for them as individuals. They can share valuable perspective and information about the visitor experience.

## INVESTING IN THE TEAM

If you want your team to feel appreciated and continue to grow and develop, you will need to invest in the tools they use in their roles as well as in their individual development.

### Professional Development

Frontline staff members are often just beginning their museum careers. Whether they hope to advance in your museum or another institution or they are content to stay in their current role, you should invest in their growth to benefit both the employees and your institution.

This investment comes in all shapes and sizes. Sometimes you need to invest time by offering expanded training related to employees' job duties and allowing them to continue to learn more advanced skills. Staff members from a variety of departments could share their expertise with the frontline staff. This expertise could be information that helps frontline staff in their current roles, such as curatorial information about the objects on display or visitor-engagement techniques to help the frontline team share stories with visitors. Staff members from other departments can also share information about their fields, their career progressions, or expertise not related to working with the public.

It also can be beneficial to bring in guest speakers from your local community. Consider experts from other museums, artists, or scholars. Community organizations could be invited to speak on specific topics, such as religious leaders sharing background information that will help staff understand the context of special exhibitions. If you have work on display relating to mental health, a local expert can talk to your team about discussing these challenging topics. Local groups that serve people with disabilities can help staff see the museum in a new way. Inviting these local experts can help your team grow their expertise and improve the experience for the groups they serve.

It's a larger investment to send frontline staff to outside professional-development opportunities such as workshops and conferences, but those opportunities should be considered. When they are possible, they can add to employees' skill sets and help employees grow in their careers. If a full conference is not possible, explore the possibility of webinars or workshops within a one-day drive. When you do send frontline staff to these events, you will want to give them information ahead of time, especially if it is their first time attending this type of event. You should set clear expectations about when they are at the event and when they return. Don't forget to include how they will pay for covered expenses, what they should wear, what they should bring with them, and what they should expect. When they return, give them the opportunity to share with the entire team what they learned.

## The Right Tools for the Job

You want to provide your team with all the tools they need to do their jobs. Start with inexpensive items such as office supplies. If a new type of pen, an organizational tray, binders, or ample sticky notes make their jobs easier, it is well worth the small expense.

They also need access to essential technical tools such as a reliable point-of-sale system, working computers, printers, and radios. Their needs will change and evolve frequently, and you should listen to them about their current needs regarding what is and isn't working. For example, they may ask you to change from a printed schedule to a scheduling application they can access on their phones. Scanners may need to be updated so they can scan tickets from visitors' phones. The more expensive changes may take time to implement, but if you are listening and making the best of what you have, the changes you can make will go a long way with your team.

The frontline team need easy ways to communicate with staff in other departments. For many museums, this communication is accomplished primarily via email. Email is how upcoming events, policy changes, staff celebrations, and institutional achievements are shared, and the frontline team should be included on those communications. Each team member should receive his or her own museum email address rather than having to use a shared departmental mailbox. Providing individual email addresses acknowledges your team members' independence, ensures they have the chance to read each message, gives them personal calendars, and allows other employees a chance to engage with each member of the frontline team.

If you use other online tools for communication or project management, be sure your team has access to those tools as well. These tools include software that allow the frontline team to report facilities needs easily and track the progress of the work orders, even if their schedules do not align with that of the facilities department. There also should be clear paths for them to complete incident reports or share information about what happens in public spaces. The other teams are relying on this information.

Employee morale is always evolving and should be carefully monitored. The way you treat and include your frontline team will have a significant impact on the team's morale, and their feedback should be carefully considered as the team continues to grow and evolve. This spirit can carry throughout your institution and lead to a true cultural change.

# 12

## Developing a Culture of Service throughout Your Museum

"Customer service is not a department."

This is a popular saying among the people I interviewed to write this book. Customer service is not a simple task or something that is the job of only the front line. It is an attitude that permeates all departments of your organization.

It's great to have a stellar visitor services team and museum store, but the success of these groups will be very limited if they don't have wider support. A true culture of service means that service is a core part of everyone's jobs. Service begins with a commitment to creating an excellent experience for visitors and focusing on how everyone in the museum contributes to that goal. If everyone isn't working together, it is visible to visitors. A true culture shift also extends beyond the visitor experience and is visible in all the museum's external relationships, including those with members, donors, volunteers, and colleagues.

Like any cultural change, developing a culture of service will take time and commitment. There is no magic pill that will make the change occur overnight. You will need to be both consistent and persistent as you move forward. That consistency will pay off and, with time, you will see the change you want to see.

As you begin to implement some of the ideas in this chapter, it's important to commit to the goal of creating a visitor-focused environment throughout your institution. This involves putting the visitor at the forefront of your decision-making processes.

### PUTTING SERVICE FRONT AND CENTER

If you want service to be part of your institution's DNA, you need to make it part of everything the institution does.

In chapter 6, we examined using your museum's mission, vision, and core values to influence your service model. Here, I challenge you to ask if those statements reflect your commitment to service and a welcoming visitor experience. Do new employees know this is a priority? Does your entire team know this is important? Is it clear to your board of trustees? The more prominent this commitment is, the more it will become a core part of who your organization is.

Start with your mission and vision statements. Are they focused on only collection care? Or do they also reflect the goal of sharing your collection with your community? You want to help your community connect to the objects that are so meaningful to your institution. Museum experiences can be powerful and deserve mention in these statements.

Next, look at your stated core values. These likely reflect your museum's commitment to collection care and scholarship as well as its goal of a vibrant, equitable workplace. Your commitment to visitors should be included here as well. If you are using one- or two-word phrases to articulate your museum's values, you might choose "service," "hospitality," "visitor-centric," "warm welcome," or something similar. If you are choosing statements, you have more room to elaborate about visitor engagement with language from your service principles.

If you want your staff to know service is a priority, something as simple as putting up signs in staff areas can have an impact. Since you are making sure service is present in your museum's mission, vision, and core values, you can post those statements in visible locations including break rooms and copy rooms and near the staff entrance. Seeing these each day can help influence steady change.

The interpretation of those statements and values will vary by role throughout the institution. Job descriptions should clearly articulate each role but often are not revised and can benefit from being updated. In addition to being in the job descriptions for frontline staff discussed in chapter 9, service should be present in descriptions throughout the institution. The phrasing should reflect the differences in how each role serves the general public, specific constituencies, or internal colleagues. For example, the job description for a curator or exhibition designer may include the responsibility to consider all visitors when creating exhibitions. Development roles may focus on building relationships with members and donors. For roles in facilities or information technology, the focus may be on internal customer service and response to work orders.

The same array of service expectations should be present in performance appraisals. These appraisals are important tools for providing feedback to employees and setting clear expectations for the future. If you use a standard form across the institution, consider adding service as a metric. Each role would have different specific execution, but the level of expectation would be consistent across the board. If you use a narrative form of evaluation, ask managers to include service in their assessments.

You also should consider how you define success. This can be challenging for museums as they are much more complex than attendance figures and profit-and-loss statements. Individual experiences matter. As you look to how and where you define success, how does service factor in? This may be what you include in your annual report, the goals you set for individual exhibitions, or updates to the board of trustees. These are places to feature changes in visitor satisfaction scores, increases in audience diversity, collaborations with community partners, and great stories from visitors.

## INVESTING IN THE FRONTLINE TEAM

One of the most powerful tools you have that can help you achieve the success mentioned above is your frontline team. These individuals are the key to your museum becoming truly visitor-focused. If you take only one thing away from this book, it should be the value of investing in your frontline team. Invest the time to carefully recruit and select the best candidates, invest time in training the team to develop their skills, invest in them as individuals, and invest in creating a structure that values their strengths and talents.

This is an investment that can feel constant and draining due to natural turnover, but that's a challenge you must embrace. If you want the best team, you will hire talented people, many at the beginning of their careers, which means they will grow with you and then move on, likely just as you've discovered their true capabilities and begun to trust in them. As difficult as it is, you must see this as a good thing. Your team is too talented to stay stagnant. That's not a frustrating thing; it's positive. Each of those talented individuals will leave a mark on your institution. They may find systematic efficiencies, have great insights they can teach others, relate to visitors in new ways that others can learn from, or be great teammates who encourage their colleagues. They also will impact numerous individual visitors during their service. They will help people connect to your collection, leaving visitors with happy memories and helping your museum achieve its mission.

In addition to investing in your frontline team, you also need to set yourself up to listen to the team. They have valuable insights that can help you in your quest to improve the experiences of visitors. Take the time to listen to them. This will help you understand visitors and consistently improve the experience for each individual.

If employees throughout the institution see a strong front line, they will begin to understand how important the visitor experience can be. If they see the valuable insights of the frontline team members, they begin to see those team members as respected colleagues. This mutual respect leads to increased collaboration, which makes everyone stronger than they are on their own.

## CROSS-DEPARTMENTAL COLLABORATION

Teams are stronger when they work together and maximize everyone's strengths. Everyone in the museum has valuable expertise, and your frontline team is no different. They are experts in people and, more specifically, your museum's visitors. They know how visitors feel when they arrive at the museum, how they move through the building, what questions they have, where they linger, where they take photographs, and where they are frustrated. They understand the nuances between different visitors and can offer valuable input in many situations.

### Inclusive Meetings and Teams

Organizations may already have several existing cross-departmental committees with focuses such as diversity and inclusion, green initiatives, and social activities. Look at each of these committees and be sure someone is included with an eye for service. If these committees don't exist at your organization, are there opportunities to create them? Bringing these groups together to focus on museum-wide tasks can foster relationships across the institution and provide great value to the museum.

As you plan for new exhibitions, installations, or programs, consider inviting more voices to the table and including someone who is focused on your museum's visitors. As you consider who to include, the logical place to start is the director of visitor services or the guest services manager. This person should be part of any project that impacts visitors or the general public. If this is your role, don't be afraid to respectfully ask to be included. Hopefully, it just hasn't occurred to your colleagues to invite you and they will welcome your participation.

As the frontline team gets stronger, this duty may be shared with others. Many members of the frontline team are early in their careers, so representing their department at an institution-wide meeting is an opportunity for professional development. Before you send them to a meeting, be sure to prep them with clear expectations and some tips on providing feedback in that setting.

Whoever represents the visitor experience will offer a different point of view from others in the room. This person can often contribute thoughts on visitor flow, clear signage, accessibility, seating, and what questions may be asked by visitors. They could mention that an object is very popular with children, so they question the decision to move it higher. There may be a particular object they believe will be touched frequently and therefore they recommend installing a low barrier in front of it. They could point out vocabulary that visitors won't be familiar with and recommend including definitions on the wall labels. They may recommend that captions be added to a video to help visitors who are deaf or hard of hearing. This person is not the only one who may contribute these thoughts, but their overall perspective is unique and should be included.

The hope is that working together in this collaborative way will help build relationships between departments that can extend beyond the conference room. When people need assistance or have questions in the future, they will solicit help from the colleagues they already know and trust.

The Chrysler Museum of Art has a core team planning each exhibition that includes a representative from each department. At least one representative from visitor services and the museum store is included in each team.

At the North Carolina Museum of Art, there is a task force within the museum focused on improving the welcoming experience and creating a more diverse environment for staff and visitors. The visitor experience team is well represented in this group.

At the Denver Museum of Nature and Science, team members are active in the museum's diversity, equity, accessibility, and inclusion efforts. Also, team members have been on hiring panels for roles in other departments, at all levels of jobs.

You likely can think of similar committees or teams in your organization. Where could frontline team members participate? Where would their insight be useful? Where could they serve that would help them understand the larger picture of museum operations?

## Internal Customer Service

The Denver Museum of Nature and Science has a wonderful saying that everyone who isn't you is your customer. This means that the high level of service you offer visitors should also be extended to your colleagues as internal customers. How do you handle requests from your colleagues? Do you respond to them in a timely manner? Do you help them achieve their goals? If service is truly an integral part of your institution, you have to prioritize service to your colleagues. This could mean forming a few simple rules for responses to colleagues or asking managers to make their own statements or rules that define internal customer service for their jobs.

The Chicago History Museum created a culture-of-service team to focus on service as a priority throughout the institution with the mission of "Supporting Each Other to Serve Our Visitors." The group is chaired by the director of visitor services and includes rotating representatives from departments across the museum. They drafted a charter and helped each department draft a practice-of-service statement that reflects the purpose, work, and service of each department. The group also hosted a series of social workshops that gathered museum staff to meet semi-informally to socialize and discuss topics of internal service to one another.

## WALKING IN THEIR SHOES

Hopefully, you respect the work of your colleagues and their contributions to the mission of your organization, but nothing will lead to more understanding than stepping into someone else's role, even for a brief period of time.

### Fulfilling Short-Term Needs

At the Denver Museum of Nature and Science, you may be surprised to discover that the person clearing your table in the café is actually a conservator. At the Chicago History Museum, a curator may greet your school group as the students exit the bus. Both museums request help from their colleagues during periods of peak visitation, such as holiday weeks and exhibition openings. Visitors will just see helpful museum workers, but the experience will be beneficial both to the frontline staff, who get much-needed assistance, and to the colleagues from other departments, who may learn things from the experience that could benefit them in their typical roles.

These opportunities usually grow out of necessity. Museum attendance is not evenly spread over the entire year. There will be days and events when you simply need more hands to get the job done. Since these needs are not consistent, it often doesn't make sense to hire a larger frontline team for these sporadic occurrences. Instead, museums turn to their broader teams for help. In addition to providing much-needed help, assisting during busy days and times increases the chance that your colleagues will feel like they made true contributions to the visitor experience. If colleagues are going to take time away from their usual tasks to assist with visitors, they want to feel useful.

Once you have determined when you could use help, choose a variety of tasks that allow everyone to feel comfortable and confident in their temporary roles. The service efforts mentioned in this book are aimed at embracing the differences among visitors and providing a variety of experiences they will enjoy. The same principles apply in these situations with colleagues. Embrace the differences among your colleagues and craft experiences they will enjoy as much as possible as they help during busy times.

Some staff members are willing to help other departments, but they chose behind-the-scenes roles as a career as they are not comfortable talking to strangers. Being asked to welcome large groups may frighten them. On the other hand, they may be comfortable running supplies to other staff members, doing light cleaning over the course of an event, or opening bottles of wine for bartenders. Someone from finance may be intimidated working in galleries but comfortable running a temporary cash register at a busy location. A curator likely feels at home in the galleries talking about content and can assist with gallery coverage. Your colleagues from special events are comfortable with people but may be scared at the prospect of answering questions about content. They would be good at greeting crowds and organizing lines. Be sure to carefully balance your needs with the skills and comfort levels of your colleagues.

### Job Shadowing

Many frontline staff members have aspirations for other positions within the museum field. They may have the talents, and perhaps the education, to qualify for many positions throughout the institution, but they don't yet have the experience. Working outside their own department will give them a better understanding of overall museum operations. This can help them as they plan for their careers as well as help them in their current roles. These experiences help them understand where their current roles fit in and how individual departments are interconnected.

At the Denver Art Museum, two employees, one from the front line and one from administration, will spend a day together. Each spends half the day working in his or her role, and the two shadow each other and share their expertise. They then present their experiences at a staff meeting so the whole team can learn more about museum operations and the roles of other departments.

Other museums consider these opportunities project by project. The work could include tasks like assisting with a program or event, moving or organizing materials, entering data, researching a topic, or creating a presentation. The frontline team is a great place to turn for a variety of temporary roles.

The type of work generally starts out basic but may grow as people show their unique talents and skills. For example, someone may first assist at a craft table during a busy family program. If that person does well, they may lead the table at a later event and direct other staff members or volunteers. If they do very well, they may be asked to design an activity for the next program. These short-term opportunities can help the diverse group of frontline employees grow within your institution and the museum field.

In addition to being professional-development opportunities for the frontline team, these activities help the other departments by bringing a fresh, visitor-centric perspective to their work and allow them to complete projects that they may not have been able to execute otherwise.

## All-Staff Training

As you develop the training program for your frontline team, consider how you could share the same training information museum-wide. Could you create an abbreviated version of the training to share with everyone? Could some material be available to all staff at their leisure? Could this be part of the onboarding process for everyone?

It can be very useful to conduct an all-staff training on customer service and what that means across the organization, but you need to be strategic. This training is not something you will be able to do often, so you should wait until you are confident in your training material. The training is ideally held at an important time, such as when you are anticipating a spike in attendance or starting an all-hands-on-deck program.

You want to make the training as brief as possible while conveying all the necessary content. Start with your service model and make sure everyone understands your key service principles, what those principles mean for the frontline team, and how the principles might apply to their jobs. Again, if you are taking them away from their duties, you want the time to be meaningful.

As you discuss the basic expectations of service, you can focus on body language, tone of voice, preparing for questions, handling unusual requests, and serving diverse visitors. If there are particular exercises that are popular in your frontline training, include them here to keep people engaged. This training can be exciting for your frontline team, who likely will enjoy the fact that others are sharing their experiences and the opportunity to be seen as the experts.

If there are specific situations that you want people to be prepared for, such as rule enforcement or being prepared for particular questions, role-playing is an excellent tool. The group is likely to include some people who are shy, so as usual, it is better to either ask for volunteers to demonstrate in front of the large group or allow everyone to practice in small groups where some people may be more comfortable. If you need people to play the role of your visitors, your frontline team likely will enjoy the opportunity to demonstrate their skills. Choose people who will have fun without being too over the top and who will be comfortable offering feedback in a positive way to others, including to those in leadership roles.

If you are not ready to host all-staff training, consider sharing portions of the training materials with the entire staff or inviting them to your training sessions. For example, if you have a curator giving a talk on a new acquisition, consider inviting everyone to attend. If you have created an online training on the history of your museum, that training could be beneficial to everyone. You also should consider providing a few slides or a handout about customer service for the onboarding training for all staff. This ensures service is present in their minds from the very beginning.

## LEADERSHIP

For many organizations, focusing on service is a momentous cultural shift, and it's difficult to make significant change in any organization without the support of the executive director and others in senior leadership roles. If this cultural change is something you believe in, you may have to work hard to inspire others to make it happen.

### Influencing Leaders

If your museum leadership isn't sure about a newly stated commitment to service, it's quite possible that you can influence them to embrace it. Few people start from a position that adamantly opposes a welcoming and inclusive visitor experience. If your leader does oppose that kind of atmosphere, you likely are already aware of that stance. In that case, it will be very challenging to change the leader's mind.

It's far more likely that service has simply never been a top priority. Museum leaders are pulled in multiple directions every day, and service may seem like something they can leave to others. They may not truly understand the benefits of a museum with an institutional culture of service. If you are able to clearly articulate the benefits of that culture, it's likely you can influence leaders' priorities.

The first step is taking the time to understand the leaders you are trying to influence. What are they passionate about? What are their short- and long-term goals? You may find this information in a strategic plan, a presentation to the board, an article the leaders wrote, or similar documents. If you aren't sure, you can simply ask about their goals and priorities.

As you learn about their goals, look for ways to connect those to service and the visitor experience. You may find a focus on diversity, equity, accessibility, and inclusion or goals relating to attendance, family visits, and community engagement. A focus on service can help your museum move forward with all these goals. Take the time to consider how your plans can help achieve leaders' goals. This will help you speak the leaders' language to demonstrate why these initiatives are important.

An important element of service is recognizing that people see the world differently. You may have to remind your leaders that some people feel uncomfortable in the museum, which may be difficult for leaders to relate to. They likely chose their career paths because of a love for their subject matter, and that probably included frequent and enjoyable visits to museums.

If you can help them understand that others start from a place of apprehension and a feeling of not belonging, they may recognize the need for an emphasis on service.

As you share your goals and perspectives, be mindful of your tone and approach. You are less likely to be successful if you speak aggressively and focus on everything that is wrong. That approach naturally makes some people defensive. Instead, focus on how things could be better. Use data whenever possible, including national data and anything you have collected in your museum. Be patient if the immediate response isn't what you are hoping for. Leaders may want time to consider your ideas. Be prepared with a few suggestions that you think would make great starting points for implementing your ideas, and see what leaders are most interested in. Ideas could include inviting someone new to a meeting, adding a step to the exhibition-review process, adding a new line to the performance-appraisal form, putting up signs about service, or creating an all-staff training. Leaders may be willing to allow you to move forward with at least one item.

## Persuading Your Team

You may find yourself on the opposite side of the situation. You may be the leader—either an executive director or a department head—who is trying to make a substantial change. In order to be successful, you need the support of your team. In this case, you have the power to establish new policies and procedures, but you also have to drive a fundamental shift in attitude.

The most important thing to remember is that it will take time. Be consistent and patient and reward good service when it occurs.

Staff members may be intimidated by these changes. You need to support your team and give them the tools they will need to be successful with new procedures and standards. In some cases, you are fundamentally changing their jobs, and that's a big adjustment. Acknowledge this as you present the new vision to your team. Be sure to compliment what they are doing well and show how you will build upon that. Articulate a clear vision with easy-to-understand expectations. Be open to feedback at all steps in the process in order to give them ownership and make them feel part of the transformation.

With any change, you may encounter some pushback, and your team members will generally fall into three categories. The first group is composed of those who support your initiatives, have the right skills to execute the new plan, and readily accept training to refine their skills. These are your allies. They likely will become the team members you turn to the most. They can help raise morale and move the team in a new direction. The only note of caution here is to be aware of perceived favoritism. It's easy to turn to them so much that you unintentionally exclude others. Be mindful of equity among the team and don't focus too much on one individual.

The second group is composed of those who are willing to make changes and learn new skills, but doing so is not natural for them. They need your time and support. They may not immediately perform at the same level as the first group, but be sure to recognize their improvement and their individual successes. It is incredibly disheartening to push oneself in new directions and then to be compared to others and told one's work still isn't good enough. Help this group do their best by offering consistent feedback and coaching. They may just become your top performers.

The last group is composed of those who will actively fight this change. They disagree with new policies and the general direction. Hopefully this is a small group, and there is still time to change their minds. If they are not meeting expectations, you want to give them every opportunity to turn their work around. Have candid discussions with them about what they are doing versus what you are expecting of them. Be clear about what is needed and be sure they feel like you believe in them and will support them. Sometimes fear of something new causes people to shut down and act out. If you can get them past their fear, they may be more open to feedback and change. If they ultimately are not able or willing to change after multiple opportunities, you will have to part ways. Do not be afraid to make that change if necessary. If you allow people with this negative attitude to stay, you may think you're being kind, but it is very hard on the team, and you must consider the team as well.

### Choosing the Right Leaders for the Team

You may need to hire new leaders at some level to oversee the frontline team. It is important that you choose people who believe in your goals and have the ability to influence others, both their team and other leaders in the organization.

They need to have strong feedback and coaching skills and be successful helping others perform to the best of their abilities. They must be able to recognize and reward great performance as well as be willing to discipline team members who aren't meeting expectations. You want leaders your frontline team can rally behind, who make them feel supported, and who can lead the team to even more success. Successful leaders of this team also enjoy and excel at helping others grow and develop in their careers, even if that means coaching people out of their department. Someone being promoted within your institution or finding a great position at another organization should be seen as a success.

You also want managers you think can work well with your leadership team. These people not only will excel within their own department but also can support the entire museum's success and truly help spread a culture of service throughout the museum.

## VISITOR FEEDBACK

Listening to visitors is a key component of improving the visitor experience. Your museum's visitors are unique, and listening to them directly can help you provide the best possible experience. You may be open to feedback but have trouble imagining what types of changes could be made based on this feedback.

These changes may be large ones, such as adding exhibitions, reorganizing galleries, changing your interpretation style, or changing operating hours. They also can include smaller changes. The Denver Museum of Nature and Science added a sign in its IMAX theater lobby that said "Trouble with stairs?" when a team member realized that the accessible entrance is available also for those who might just not want to or be able to handle the steep stairs in the theater. At the Denver Art Museum, visitors were consistently asking about the frames in the nineteenth-century galleries, so when the galleries were reinstalled, more information about the frames was added to the didactics.

The Chrysler Museum of Art engaged a focus group while planning a new interactive children's gallery. The museum received a lot of useful feedback, but one of the most useful items had nothing to do with the content or the activities. It was about the door. Staff planned to have the door propped open, as they thought that was a welcoming gesture and would invite families in. Parents stated very clearly that they preferred the door remain closed. They felt more secure and could enjoy their visits much more if their children were confined to the area. This small change made a big impact on these visitors.

## COMMUNITY ENGAGEMENT

The majority of this book has been focused on the visitor experience within your museum, and that is essential, but as you prioritize the needs and desires of your visitors, it's also important to look beyond your walls. If you truly want to connect to your community, you will have to reach out to those who are not currently visiting your museum.

You may have an individual or a department focusing on community engagement, but there are many ways that these initiatives overlap with the visitor experience efforts and team. As mentioned previously, one of the primary reasons that people don't visit museums is that they don't see museums as places for people like them. This can be a challenging barrier to overcome and a difficult perception to change. One way to break through this barrier is to partner with community groups in which people do feel like they belong.

The goal with initiatives such as this is to build genuine relationships with community groups, particularly those that represent currently underrepresented groups at your museum. You may choose to partner with community organizations such as the National Urban League, your local Pride organization, groups that serve teenagers from underserved communities, and many others that are serving the people you want to encourage to visit.

The best way to build sincere relationships with these groups is to meet them where they are. You can't expect them to change to fit your needs. You need to listen and determine how you can partner in ways that work for them. For example, if you offer to host a group's monthly meetings and they have been meeting on Tuesdays for years, they may not be willing to move the meetings to Thursdays simply because it works better for you. You need to show that you sincerely want to welcome them, and you should be as flexible as you can. In another example, they may want to sponsor a performance at your institution. They may design their program in a completely different way from how the museum would, but again, you need to be as flexible as possible and find something that works for everyone rather than try to force them to do things your way. If you aren't sure how to start reaching out to these groups, you can use your existing programming as an invitation to them. This may include evening programs, family days, or programs in the museum store like the one shown in figure 12.1.

You need to avoid looking for a perfectly reciprocal relationship. You are not doing these groups favors by giving them space for meetings, offering discounts for programs, or providing speakers for their events. These actions are benefiting your museum. You are taking a step toward helping their group members feel welcome in your institution.

You can also ask community groups to advise you regarding upcoming programs or exhibitions. For example, if you have an upcoming exhibition that includes information about enslaved servants, you may want to reach out to local African American organizations as well as local historians. While those groups will share information that is useful for all departments and will help with exhibition design and programming, they will also share information that is useful to the frontline team. This may include preferred language or language to avoid, areas in which visitors may want to give feedback or respond, or stories staff should focus on sharing. During the planning for a similar exhibition, one museum learned that the craftsmanship demonstrated by the enslaved servants and the servants' advanced technical skills were very important to feature, so the frontline staff was happy to learn and share those stories. This sharing of advice and information makes your exhibitions, and the visitor experience in the exhibitions, stronger.

As you engage these groups, you need to be sure that this is not a one-time invitation. It will take multiple interactions for your relationship to grow and for trust to build. When done cor-

**Figure 12.1.** *Source: North Carolina Museum of Art*

rectly and sincerely, this type of engagement can help with long-term audience development and visitor experience goals. However, these community initiatives won't work if you haven't created a welcoming environment in your museum. If the visitor experience is poor, you are likely to see these folks only one time. Your museum will not become a part of their lives.

You can't achieve your mission without visitors. Without them, your museum is simply a vault full of wonderful objects and exhibitions. You must take the time to learn about your museum's visitors, understand their motivations and preferences, and adapt your service to meet their needs. In order to be successful, you will need to build a strong frontline team and a culture of service throughout the institution.

# Index

125

# About the Author

**Colleen Higginbotham** is the deputy director for visitor experience at the Chrysler Museum of Art in Norfolk, Virginia. She has more than twenty-five years of customer-service management experience and is passionate about creating individual experiences and matching the right service to the right visitor. She believes in embracing the differences in each visitor and customizing experiences based on the visitor's background, motivations, experience, abilities, and preferences.

In 2007, she implemented the museum's gallery-host program, which blends the roles of security and service in the public galleries. The talented gallery hosts provide visitors with a warm welcome, ensure the safety of the collection, answer questions, and engage visitors in casual conversations about art.

Beyond serving as a leader in her own institution, she has served the museum industry through multiple conference presentations with the American Alliance of Museums, Museum Store Association, Visitor Experience Group, and Virginia Association of Museums. She has also served as a peer reviewer for the Museum Assessment Program through the American Alliance of Museums and as a board member for the Museum Store Association.